Laurel Hill Cemetery *of* *Saco, Maine*

LAUREL HILL CEMETERY *of* SACO, MAINE

LESLIE ROUNDS AND EMORY ROUNDS
ON BEHALF OF THE DYER LIBRARY ASSOCIATION

THE History PRESS

Published by The History Press
Charleston, SC
www.historypress.net

First published 2018

Manufactured in the United States

ISBN 9781467139977

Library of Congress Control Number: 2017963923

CONTENTS

AN INTERESTING PLACE OF RESORT

On July 18, 1844, the trustees of the Laurel Hill Cemetery met in a Saco Main Street law office to sign the papers to begin construction of the new burial ground. The land where it would be located had been bought that spring for $600 with the very practical guarantee that John Fairfield, the seller, "shall take the crops the present season."

By 1849, the trustees (with a bit of pride) were advertising that the cemetery was based on

> *the modern plan of Mount Auburn and others, whereby families can be accommodated with private lots, which they can make up and ornament according to their own taste, and for this purpose, a beautiful lot of about 25 acres of land, in Saco, was purchased lying on the handsome swell, next to and adjoining the late Gov. Fairfield's farm. The grounds were laid out by Waldo Higginson, Esq. an experienced engineer. There have been many trees set out upon the avenues and paths, and a receiving tomb erected, and about 150 private lots have been taken. This cemetery is already becoming an interesting place of resort, and is becoming more so, as the number of private lots increases, and the improvements progress.*

In the town's earliest days—in the late seventeenth and early eighteenth centuries—many of Saco's dead were buried at a cemetery not far from the banks of the Saco River, about a half mile closer to the Atlantic Ocean than Laurel Hill. This cemetery, now called Rendezvous Point, was inconveniently

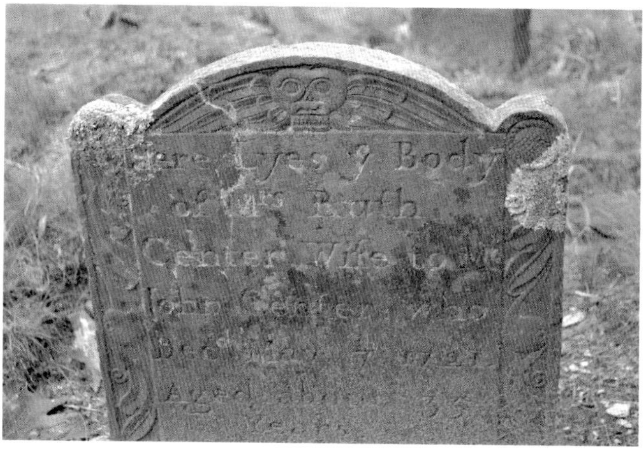

A typical eighteenth-century gravestone, one of the few remaining headstones in the burying ground at Rendezvous Point. *Authors' collection.*

far from the center of the growing village. By about 1760, some people were being interred on a small plot of land next to the Unitarian Church that Sir William Pepperrell, one of the largest landowners in the area, had donated to the town (called, for a while, Pepperrellborough). Although Sir William died in 1759 and bequeathed to the town additional land for the cemetery, legal issues arose, and that land didn't formally change hands until 1798. By that time, however, the Pepperrell burying ground was the final resting place for quite a few of Saco's former residents.

These first two of Saco's burying grounds, like all of their era, were places of admonition. One of the most common of epitaphs chiseled into eighteenth-century headstones was this, or one of its many similar variations:

> *Remember friends, as you pass by*
> *As you are now so once was I*
> *As I am now so you shall be*
> *Prepare for death and follow me.*

In addition to this dark warning, the headstones of the era featured grim death's heads that were often in the form of leering skulls (occasionally sprouting somewhat more promising wings). Gravestones of the time were nearly always carved of slate, which was widely available around New England, but the material ranged in color from gray to near black. These closely spaced, dark-colored gravestones gave cemeteries an ominous appearance.

By the beginning of the nineteenth century, religious views in New England had evolved from the Puritans' rigid plan of predestination (some small group of people were God's elect, but everyone else—the vast majority—was among those who had not been, and would not be, chosen by God for salvation). In this Calvinistic view, even babies were doomed if they weren't already predestined to be saved.

Now, however, people began to believe that their own good works *could* lead them on the path to heaven. As this more hopeful outlook began influencing culture, gravestones began to change as well: death's heads evolved into winged angel's faces and then even less suggestive weeping willows. This wasn't to say that death didn't remain an ever-present fear. To the contrary, for children in the nineteenth century, the mortality rate began to rise over its previous high level, and few families managed to raise a brood without losing some to disease or accidents. There were no effective treatments for the numerous contagious illnesses that wracked people's lives and often caused their swift deaths. Nevertheless, the prevailing attitude toward death was changing.

Early in the nineteenth century, many stonecutters started to work with the marble that was now being excavated in open quarries, especially in Vermont. As the railroads bound New England together, the marble could be easily shipped, making it readily available even far from the quarries. It was immediately popular. Stonecutters found that it was easier to work with than slate since it was a "softer" stone, and customers appreciated its ethereal—even hopeful—white color. It would be well into the next century before people realized that these same marble stones all but melted under the onslaught of a harsh environment.

Near the end of the century, granite was introduced. It is harder than marble and could be polished to an attractive shine. Improved tools and techniques made it possible to carve this stone, but by the time it was introduced, a new, more minimalist style had begun to gain ground. Long epitaphs, and even the details of birth and death dates, were vanishing. Often, just a last name, first initial and year of birth or even just a death date would be all that was included.

In the late 1820s, as the men at the forefront of a new cemetery movement began planning for Mount Auburn Cemetery in Cambridge, Massachusetts, several new notions came into play. There was a desire to create a cemetery where great men's monuments would be seen and visited by the unenlightened public and thus, it was hoped, inspire them to emulate greatness. A horticultural movement based on England's lovely private gardens had sprung up in recent decades; the new cemetery could be a place to display *American* horticultural skill. There was also a rising awareness that overfilled urban graveyards might be a source of "miasmas" (deathly, invisible fumes), which were thought to sicken and even kill those in the area. (As it happened, this wasn't as far off the mark as it might seem, since public water supplies could be contaminated by the profusion of shallowly buried, decaying corpses.) Land was soon purchased and landscaped, and lots were put up for sale. The presence of nature at the cemetery had the effect of sweetening bitter loss—or so the planners claimed. Soon, other cemeteries styled after Mount Auburn began to open in urban areas. Laurel Hill Cemetery was created to offer a Mount Auburn–like experience to Mainers.

In Saco, Josiah Calef, Esq., was chosen to be the chairman of the new board of trustees. The original lots were sold for $14.33. Money for managing the new cemetery was tight. There were many expenses involved in laying out the avenues and paths that crisscrossed the original plot of land. Trees had to be planted in what had been an open hayfield. Still, planning ahead, the trustees soon bought two adjoining plots of land, one for $55.00 and a larger one for $933.53 in 1845. In 1846, Calef reported to the board, "The manager is happy to find that the cemetery is constantly gaining popularity and fame and is becoming a favorite walk, and visitors have generally been indisposed to do acts of violence or indiscretion in or about the Cemetery. And if the trees that have been set should do well, the acorns and nuts and shrubbery that have been planted should prosper, and if good taste should be manifested by the proprietors of Lots, the time cannot be very distant when on many accounts this will be esteemed a most interesting place."

Still, he also reported that a receiving tomb—a building to hold the bodies of those who died over the winter, when the ground was too frozen to inter them—was desperately needed, as many people had complained of the lack of one. There was some thought that a tomb might be available elsewhere that could be moved and reused, so the expensive project was put off for a few years. But none could be found, so in 1849, the trustees "built a capacious Tomb" at a cost of $414.78. In 1850, Calef reported his disappointment that they "have not made so extensive improvements in and about the cemetery as they would have been glad to have done, if they had received funds from the sale of Lots to justify it. But it will be recollected that a large outlay had been made for supplying a receiving Tomb and other improvements the year previous to this." The only major outlay of cash that year was for $24.75 to purchase sleigh runners that could replace the wheels of the hearse in wintertime. The sale of lots must have improved, as the cemetery's financial situation rapidly strengthened afterward.

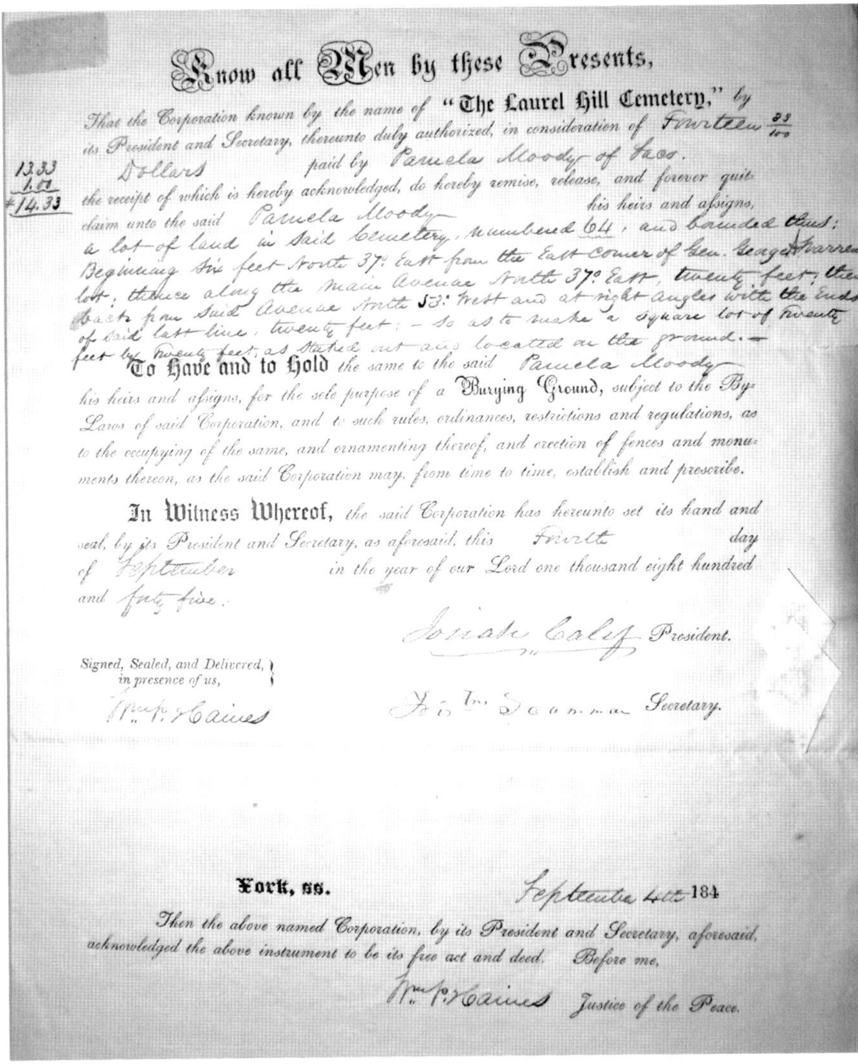

Know all Men by these Presents,

That the Corporation known by the name of "The Laurel Hill Cemetery," by its President and Secretary, thereunto duly authorized, in consideration of Fourteen 33/100 Dollars paid by Pamela Moody of Saco. the receipt of which is hereby acknowledged, do hereby remise, release, and forever quit-claim unto the said Pamela Moody his heirs and assigns, a lot of land in said Cemetery, numbered 64, and bounded thus: Beginning six feet North 37° East from the East corner of Gen. George Warren's lot; thence along the main Avenue North 37° East, twenty feet; then back from said Avenue North 53° West and at right angles with the ends of said last line, twenty feet; – so as to make a square lot of twenty feet by twenty feet, as staked out and located on the ground.—

13.33
1.00
$14.33

To Have and to Hold the same to the said Pamela Moody his heirs and assigns, for the sole purpose of a Burying Ground, subject to the By-Laws of said Corporation, and to such rules, ordinances, restrictions and regulations, as to the occupying of the same, and ornamenting thereof, and erection of fences and monuments thereon, as the said Corporation may, from time to time, establish and prescribe.

In Witness Whereof, the said Corporation has hereunto set its hand and seal, by its President and Secretary, as aforesaid, this Fourth day of September in the year of our Lord one thousand eight hundred and forty five.

Josiah Calef President.

Signed, Sealed, and Delivered, in presence of us,

Wm. P. Haines

Jos. Wm. Seaman Secretary.

York, ss. September 4th 184

Then the above named Corporation, by its President and Secretary, aforesaid, acknowledged the above instrument to be its free act and deed. Before me,

Wm. P. Haines Justice of the Peace.

Laurel Hill Cemetery was just one year old when Pamela Moody purchased a plot for $14.33 and received this deed. *Collection of Dyer Library/Saco Museum.*

Around this time, some local families began choosing to relocate their departed relatives from the Pepperrell burying ground. The dead (at least those who had living relatives with the funds to purchase lots in Laurel Hill) were transferred to the bucolic new cemetery. Everyone else was left behind, and Pepperrell burying ground, now less visited, suffered from a gradual neglect. Pepperrell certainly wasn't the only source of transfers to the new cemetery, however. There are about 317 gravestones in Laurel Hill Cemetery that bear death dates that precede the founding of the cemetery.

The vast majority of these are located in family plots that also include people who died after the cemetery was founded. Quite likely, some of these earlier gravestones are just memorial markers; the dead were left behind in family plots of other, less attractive cemeteries, but the stones were moved to the new plots. The early-date stones are scattered all across the oldest part of the cemetery—a large area—but are much too widely separated to represent original burials that occurred in the farm field before the cemetery was founded there, a story that has often been repeated to explain their presence.

By the early twentieth century, with additional funding, the cemetery began a program of further design and landscaping. In particular, the well-to-do Deering family became involved in leadership of the cemetery. Arthur Shurcliff, a Boston landscape architect (who had also had a hand in designing Colonial Williamsburg and Old Sturbridge Village), was hired to update the grounds. Shurcliff decided that the cemetery should be an arboretum as well as a burial place. His input led to a massive replacement of the numerous paths that had crisscrossed the cemetery with a network of about seven miles of paved lanes. Although the former paths were filled with topsoil to bring them up to ground level, it's still possible to spot some of their locations based on the layout of graves.

In 1937, when Elizabeth Rice became the last of her immediate family to die, she gave a very large bequest to the cemetery in memory of her father and one of her brothers. Some of that money was used to fund a new drainage system and the installation of underground cast-iron water pipes throughout the cemetery. Continuing the development of Laurel Hill's new arboretum role, thirty-five copper beech trees were imported from Belgium, probably in about 1969. As Ralph Hawkes, a former board president, recalled to a newspaper reporter in 1982, the shipments of the expensive trees, one after another, were caught up in customs red tape and the trees died on the docks.

Today, Laurel Hill features about one hundred acres that are maintained and another seventy acres that aren't landscaped. It's estimated that more than fifty thousand people may be buried there. In 1989, groundskeeper William Tate reported that there were more than a million naturalized daffodils planted. Since the daffodils are allowed to propagate naturally, and ten thousand more are added each year, that number must surely have

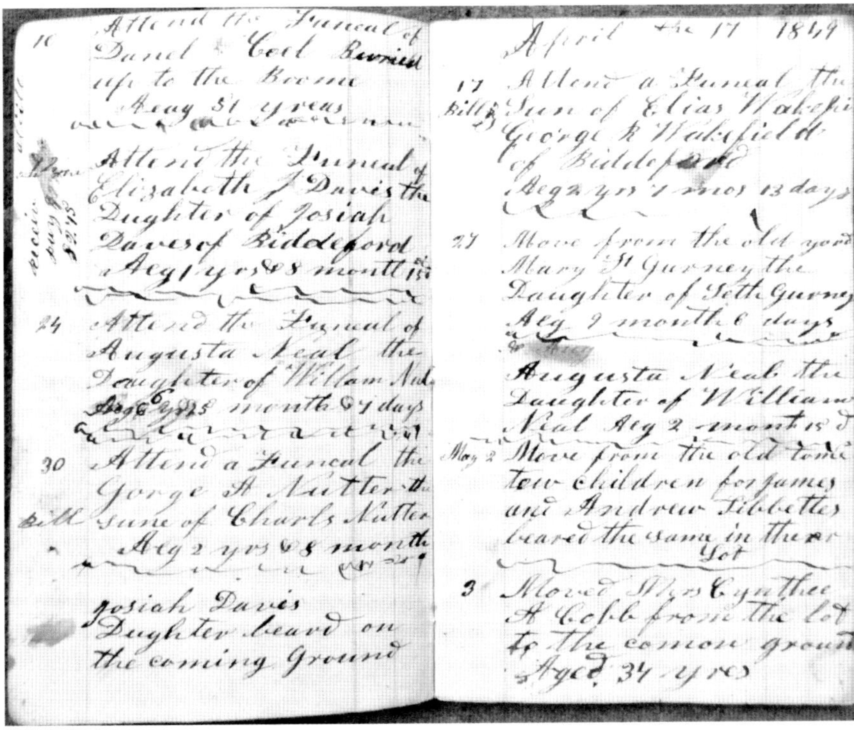

10 Attend the Funeral of
Danel Coel Buried
up to the Broome
Aeg 31 years

Attend the Funeral of
Elizabeth J Davis the
Dughter of Josiah
Daves of Biddeford
Aeg 1 yrs & 8 month 15 d

24 Attend the Funeral of
Augusta Neal the
Daughter of William Neal
Aeg 6 yrs 5 month & 7 days

30 Attend a Funeral the
Gorge A Nutter the
Sune of Charls Nutter
Aeg 2 yrs & 8 month

Josiah Davis
Dughter beard on
the coming Ground

April the 17 1849

17 Attend a Funeral the
Sun of Elias Wakefi
George R Wakefield
of Biddeford
Aeg 2 yrs 7 mos 13 days

27 Move from the old yard
Mary H Gurney the
Daughter of Seth Gurney
Aeg 9 month 6 days

Augusta Neal the
Daughter of William
Neal Aeg 2 month 15 d

May 2 Move from the old tomb
tow children for James
and Andrew Tibbetts
beared the same in their
Lot

3 Moved Mrs Cynthia
A Cobb from the lot
to the comon ground
Aged 34 yrs

A ledger that records funerals, burials and a few occasions when the deceased were moved from other locations. *Collection of Laurel Hill Cemetery.*

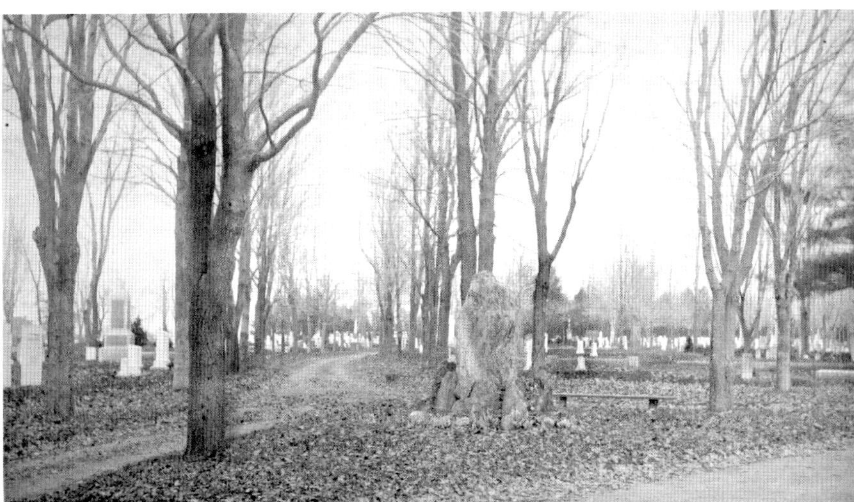

A late nineteenth-century view looking up Main Avenue toward Beach Street. It was easier to decorate with rocks than remove them. *Collection of Laurel Hill Cemetery.*

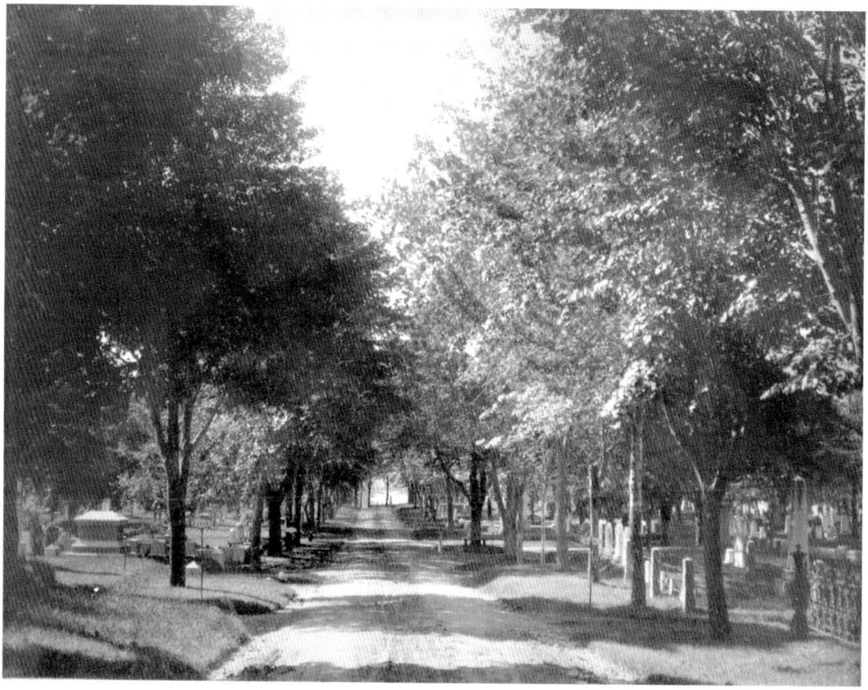

A vintage image looking toward the Saco River, with the river clearly in view. Several plots include fences. *Collection of Laurel Hill Cemetery.*

soared since then. The cemetery also has numerous lilies, tulips and lilacs, all drawing visitors to enjoy the springtime splendor. It features about one hundred varieties of European and American trees that aren't native to Maine, as well as numerous native species.

The cemetery is now a top choice for prom photographs, and the chapel is frequently used for weddings. The shady lanes are in constant use by walkers and joggers. Josiah Calef's vision of the cemetery as an "interesting place of resort" has been completely embraced by people in the area, yet few who stroll here know the stories behind the graves they pass. The brief tales that follow are arranged by the location of the graves, street by street. At the beginning of each biography is the information on the plot that was included in *York County Cemetery Inscriptions*, a set of four books that was the result of a massive project that began in the late 1950s to transcribe all the gravestones in the county. When the Laurel Hill graves were transcribed, many of the stones were in significantly better condition than they are now. In many cases, engraved text that is now little more than a blur was still

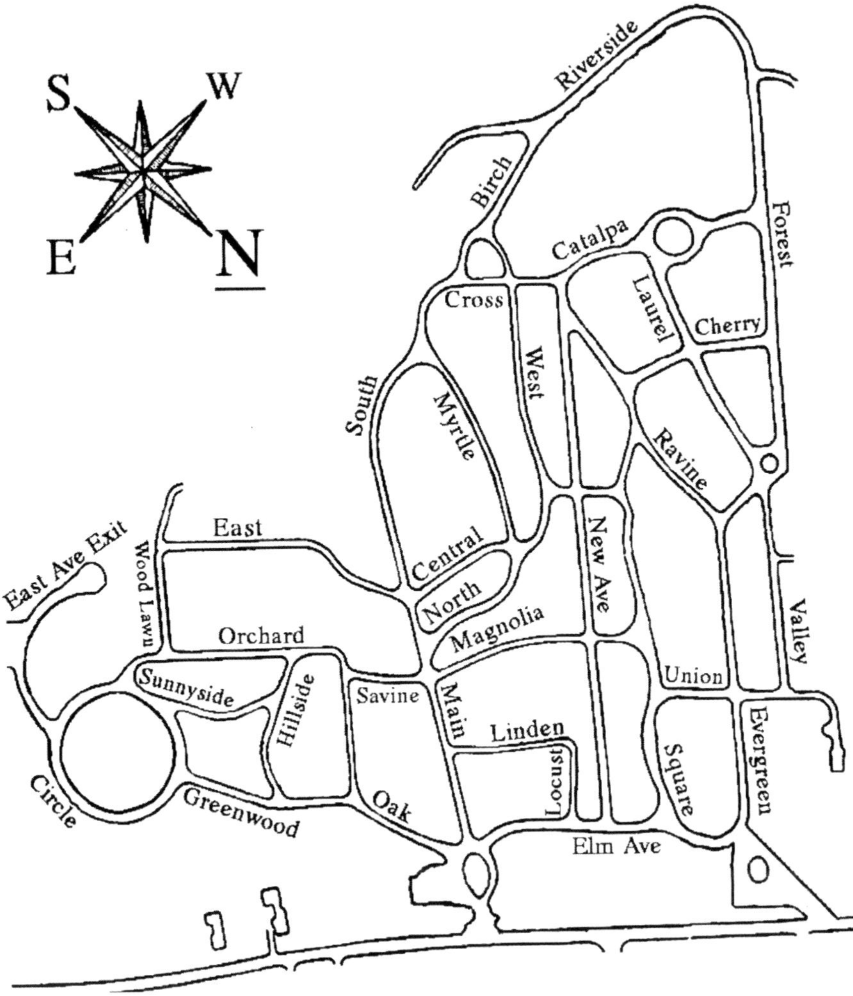

A map of Laurel Hill Cemetery. *Authors' collection.*

readable more than a half century before. Although the transcriptions are nearly always accurate, not surprisingly, given the sheer volume of work, some of the names and dates were found to be erroneous. Those errors are noted in the biographies.

EVERGREEN AVENUE

DOLLIFF, F.P., 21 NOV. 1853–2 FEB. 1855
S.A., 21 NOV. 1851–8 JUNE 1899
S., 25 JAN. 1821–31 JULY 1901
N.C., 3 MARCH 1817–26 APR 1891
A.L., 20 OCT. 1848–20 NOV. 1930
O.D., 27 MARCH 1837–24 JULY 1884

The Dolliff plot features a large central monument, elaborate steps and individual markers for each family member that carry just their initials and dates of birth and death, in keeping with the new style of the time. Buried here are Samuel Dolliff, born in 1821, who worked as a house carpenter in Biddeford; his wife, Nancy; their daughter, Ann L., who became a dressmaker; and their son, Octavius, who worked as a store clerk. In 1872, there was another addition to the Dolliff family when Ann gave birth to little Belle, apparently out of wedlock. In 1900, the census shows Samuel living with Annie and Belle, who was teaching school. Just a few months later, Belle married a New Hampshire man, Fred Drew. Drew was a train engineer, and Belle settled with him in Camp Ellis. They don't seem to have had any children. In the back side of the plot are Samuel and Nancy's daughter, Almira, who married then quickly divorced; their son, Samuel, who died in early adulthood; and a child who lived for less than two years and whose name wasn't recorded in Biddeford's vital records but fortunately was named in the newspaper as Franklin P. Dolliff.

The Dolliffs are buried alongside a lane that's deeply shaded by large red and sugar maple trees. At one time, the cemetery included at least one of each type of tree that was native to this part of Maine. These maples reflect that use of local species.

Scattered throughout the cemetery are two types of large, red-leafed trees. The more upright variety is a hybrid version of the silver maple called a Crimson King maple. Silver maples are fast-growing shade trees but have weak wood that's easily damaged in high winds. Worse, Crimson Kings drop seed pods that readily grow in Maine and compete with native species. Long after Laurel Hill's Crimson Kings were planted, the sale of this variety was banned in Maine as an invasive, nonnative species. The other red-leafed trees are the much more desirable copper beech trees. Copper beeches are slow growing and become huge shade trees with attractive silvery trunks and foliage that stands out in the landscape.

LOW, GEORGE M., D. 20 NOV 1897, AGED 70 YRS. 2 MOS.
SARAH C., DAU. OF THOMAS AND LYDIA LOW, D. 7 DEC 1843, AGED 22 YRS.
THOMAS, D. 25 MARCH 1848, AGED 60 YRS.
LYDIA, WIFE OF THOMAS LOW, D. 15 DEC 1852, AGED 63 YRS.

Thomas Low was probably the son of Thomas Low of Lyman. His wife, Lydia, was the daughter of Samuel Gooch and Betsey Emery of Wells. At least by 1840, the couple lived in Kennebunk, Maine, making the choice of Laurel Hill Cemetery an interesting one, both because neither of them had any significant ties to Saco and because Kennebunk also has an attractive, park-like cemetery. By the time of the 1850 census, Thomas Low and his daughter, Sarah, had already died. Lydia was still living in Kennebunk with her surviving children Samuel, Thomas, George and Francis, as well as Samuel's wife, Sophia Huff, and their three children, with three yet to be born—a very crowded household! All of Lydia's sons followed the same career path as their father: they were joiners, or furniture makers. Some of the Low graves face the current avenue, and some face the opposite way. This positioning reflects the fact that, early on, there were many paths through the graves. Sarah's grave faces toward one of these forgotten lanes.

Stones that are essentially identical to the Lows' appear in cemeteries all over York County, becoming more common toward the southwest. Since slate is a very hard stone, it has held up well under the onslaught of acid rain that has so badly eroded marble stones. Nearly all feature decorative

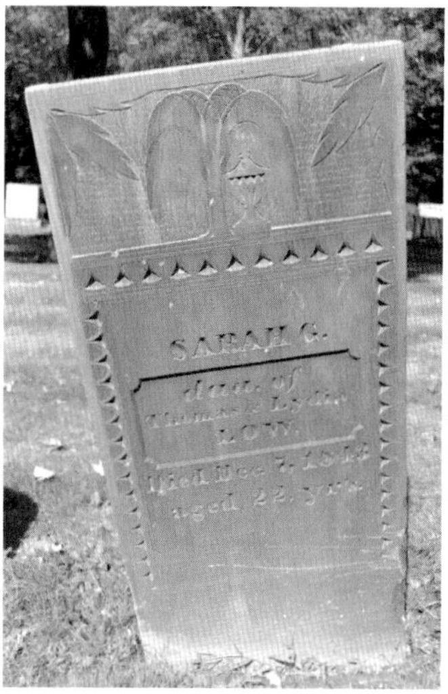

The headstone of Sarah Low, likely carved by Timothy Eastman. *Authors' collection.*

crosshatching carved into the tops and sides. Crosshatching was a popular form of decorative work, especially in northeastern Massachusetts, and there were several carvers using it to embellish their stones. In Hope Cemetery in Kennebunk, one of the stones that closely resembles the Low stones in decoration and in shape is signed on the lower back with "T. Eastman, Exeter." Eastman may also be the source for the Low stones, since they share many common elements with others he signed.

Timothy Goodhue Eastman was the son of Joseph Eastman and Sally Prescott. He was born in Deerfield, New Hampshire, in 1804. He married Abigail Hall. They were the parents of at least seven children, one of whom died unnamed just four days after birth. Timothy, on the 1850 census, was listed as a stone carver. He died very shortly after the census was taken, on July 15, 1850. His death notice says that he died of consumption, but it's also possible that he was killed by "stone carver's disease," a chronic obstructive pulmonary disease that was caused by inhaling the dust that stonecutting created. His wife died just two years later.

INGERSOLL, RICHMOND H., 1834–1913. ERECTED BY THE GRAND LODGE, KNIGHTS OF PYTHIAS OF MAINE, IN MEMORY OF ITS FIRST GRAND CHANCELLOR. [FATHER]
MARCIA M., [MOTHER], 1840–1930

On the 1860 census, Richmond Ingersoll was a merchant in Portland. By 1870, he was living in Biddeford and working as a bank cashier, and he later served as the treasurer of a bank for nearly the rest of his life. In 1860, he married Marcia M. Atkinson of Biddeford. They set up housekeeping there, first in a large rooming house but later in their own home on Crescent Street. They would become parents to six children, starting with twins Minnie and Clinton in 1861. Sadly, by 1900, there was only one child left alive. Clinton died shortly after birth, as did his brother Eugene in 1868.

Frederick, born in 1863, died at the age of three. Minnie lived until just 1888. Only Anna, born in 1874, would survive into adulthood; she lived to the age of ninety-eight and never married. Richmond was an important member of the Knights of Pythias Fraternal Order, which was founded in 1864 in Washington, D.C., by Justus Rathbone, who wanted to "rekindle brotherly sentiment throughout the land." In the nineteenth century, fraternal orders were hugely popular. Many men belonged to at least one, but some joined a half dozen or more. There are numerous stones in the cemetery that note membership in fraternal orders. The Knights of Pythias still has about fifty thousand members in about two thousand lodges.

MASON, JEREMIAH M., HOLLIS, 28 MARCH 1820–LIMERICK, 20 MARCH 1897
MARTHA W. WOODMAN, WIFE OF JEREMIAH M. MASON, BUXTON, 10 FEB 1824–23 MARCH 1891
MARTHA B., LIMERICK, 24 SEP 1855–LIMERICK, 17 MARCH 1927
WILLIAM W., LIMERICK, 25 AUG 1851–PORTLAND, 14 JAN 1938
MARY S. CLEAVES, WIFE OF WILLIAM W. MASON, B. IN BRIDGTON, D. IN PORTLAND, 17 MARCH 1930

Jeremiah Mason was born in Hollis but moved to Limerick, where, according to the 1870 census, he was operating a dry goods store. His personal property and real estate were valued at a total of $8,000, a large amount for the time. He and Martha had at least four children: William; Martha ("Mattie"); June, born in 1860; and Frances ("Frannie"), born in 1861. In 1870, Jeremiah's son, William, was working as a clerk in his father's store, and in 1880, he was listed as a merchant and had a live-in servant from Sweden. William married

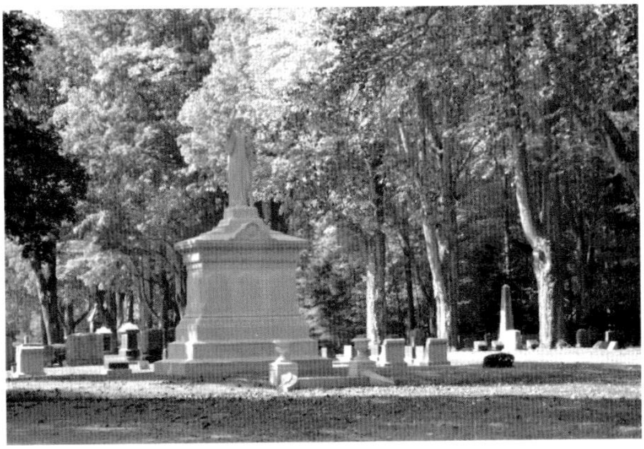

Jeremiah Mason's impressive Cleaves angel. *Authors' collection.*

Mary S. Cleaves of Bridgton. Whether or not his wife was related to Charles H. Cleaves, a well-known gravestone carver of Saco for many years and also the artist who sculpted the angel pictured here is unknown. Just in case there were any doubts about the Mason family's eventual fate, the angel points decisively heavenward.

Charles Cleaves was the son of Ann and Harrison Cleaves. First Harrison, and then Charles, operated a gravestone business on Main Street in Saco that lasted for about ninety years. Charles's monumental fancywork like this is well known, but he surely was also responsible for many of the simpler stones in Laurel Hill.

VALLEY AND FOREST AVENUES

UMER, ARIF, CO. BRULSEN, TURKEY, ALBANIAN MUHAMMEDAN, L. 3 SEPT 1893–V. 12 JAN 1910
ETEM, BESIM, CO. BILISLD, TURKEY, ALBANIAN MUHAMMEDAN, L. 19 APR 1890–V. 12 JAN 1910

Arif and Besim came to Maine around 1907 and found jobs in a textile mill. The young men were cousins; they had a pair of uncles who lived in Biddeford, but not long before their deaths, Arif and Besim had relocated to Saco and were living in an apartment in the back of the York Institute block, near the river and railroad tracks.

According to a newspaper account, at about 6:40 p.m. the two were cutting across the railroad tracks, carrying a few letters to a relative in Biddeford. Two trains were passing: the American Express no. 174 and a much slower freight train. In an all-too-common railroading accident, the noise of the departing freight masked the sound of the oncoming express, and the young men were both struck and killed instantly.

The engineer telegraphed back to Saco (the express didn't stop, of course) to notify the stationmaster that he was soaked with blood and that he believed he'd hit someone. Men who went out with lanterns to investigate quickly found the body of a large young man. It was only when they spotted another cap, "like those worn by the Greeks," that they suspected there might be a second victim. He was soon located. That man, the smaller of the pair, had been dismembered, a situation that was described in graphic detail in the front-page newspaper coverage. The two were brought to the cellar of the local coroner and undertaker, where it was discovered that the smaller man—whomever he was—had been carrying a considerable amount of money carefully stitched into his belt for safekeeping. It was a time of great prejudice against immigrants, and the newspaper fed the public's cravings: "The fatality created the greatest excitement among the Greeks and Albanians and other foreigners who have located to the two cities, hundreds swarming to the railroad yards as soon as they learned of the accident, the police finally being compelled to disperse the excited dark-skinned sons of Greece."

At this time, Greeks and Turks, both included in the crumbling Ottoman Empire, were sharply divided by Turkish aggression, fueled by a drive toward statehood that frequently ended with Greeks on the losing side. If a crowd of "Greek" immigrants turned out, it's doubtful they were there to mourn the loss of these two young men. However, a search of the census for 1910 shows that there were many large boardinghouses, especially in Biddeford, that were home to numerous young, single, male Turkish or Albanian immigrants, most of whom had arrived about the same time as Arif and Besim. It may well have been this group—rather than Greeks—that turned out to learn more of the deaths of their young compatriots. A funeral service was held the next morning in the rooms of the undertaker, and the cousins were laid to rest with their graves facing into the woods. This appears to isolate them from other burials, but it's also possible that they're facing in the direction of Mecca, in respect for their faith. The towns of their origin engraved on their stones (the actual spelling on the graves appears to be "Bratsan" and "Bitista") don't correspond with any known place names. Most likely the names were supplied, in uncertain English, by their Biddeford relatives and the carver guessed at their spelling.

Dubois, Narcisse, b. in Paris, France, 13 Oct 1832, d. 27 Dec 1907
Charles, 13 Oct 1870–23 Feb 1930
Arthur, son of Charles and Alexsina Dubois, 30 Aug 1904–22 Nov 1910
Elizabeth, dau. of Charles and Alexsina Dubois, 26 July 1902–26 Nov 1910
Florida, 12 Aug 1898–27 Nov 1910
Louise, 12 May 1876–13 April 1919
Tavoularis, Elizabeth [Mother], 27 Nov 1880–2 Aug 1960

The 1910 census, taken on April 15, captures a moment in time before the Dubois household was struck with unspeakable tragedy. Charles, forty, from Massachusetts, and his wife, Alexsina (who was born Eugenie Frechette), thirty-seven, from Montreal, were the parents of eight living children and one who had already passed away. Charles, the son of Paris-born Narcisse, was a supervisor in a cotton mill. Louise and Elizabeth (who married Peter Tavoularis in 1910) were Charles's younger sisters, both of whom also worked in the mills. Living with them at 20 Pleasant Street in Saco were George, fourteen; Florida, twelve; Alice, ten; Elizabeth, eight; Arthur, five; Henry, three; and little Ada, who was just one month old. The following November, Florida, Elizabeth and Arthur would all die of scarlet fever within a five-day period.

Even well into the twentieth century, this scourge—a more severe and highly contagious form of "strep throat"—would continue to kill children, often several in a family. It wasn't until penicillin was introduced at the conclusion of World War II that scarlet fever's lethal potential was curbed. Still, most children who developed scarlet fever would recover; it was only the minority who were so ill that they developed sepsis—blood poisoning—and died. Children at this time were much more likely to die of diphtheria, whooping cough and tuberculosis ("consumption"), all-too-common illnesses of the era.

LAUREL AVENUE

HILL, HAMPTON E., M.D. [FATHER], D. 9 JAN 1894 AGED 43 YRS. 8 MOS. 19 DAYS
MYRA E. [MOTHER], D. 21 OCT 1891, AGED 38 YRS. 8 MOS.
HOVEY H., 10 APR 1876–5 DEC 1924
PAUL S., 1881–1947
HILL, PAUL, 23 SEPT 1906–24 SEPT. 1985
CLARE C. MATTHEWS, HIS WIFE,
HILL, JOHN H. [FATHER], 1826–1907
DORCAS A. LOCKE [MOTHER], WIFE OF JOHN H. HILL, 1829–1906
J. FRANK, 1855–1930

On December 9, 1945, General George Patton was driven out into the countryside in Germany so that he could hunt pheasants. The general's car was involved in a minor accident, but Patton was thrust forward in his seat (in a time long before seatbelts were common), struck his head and broke his neck. Paralyzed, he was quickly evacuated to an army emergency room in Heidelberg, where army surgeon Dr. Paul S. Hill Jr. attended him. Patton died there on the twenty-first. After the war, Paul Jr. returned to Saco, where he managed his private practice as well as a Biddeford hospital. He was very actively involved with his high school alma mater, Thornton Academy, and the stadium there is named after him. Hill's father, Paul S. Hill, was a general practice physician in Biddeford who relocated to Saco in about 1920. The family was doing well enough economically to have a live-in servant, but they also had a boarder—a seeming contradiction that wasn't that uncommon, as it turns out. Many people, being very practical, took in boarders even if they didn't need the additional money. Paul Sr.'s father was Hampton E. Hill, also a physician and surgeon. The curious cause of his early death in 1894 was listed as "softening of the brain." Hampton's parents—John Hill, a farmer, and his wife, Dorcas Locke—and their other son, J. Frank, are also buried in this plot.

MCKENNEY, SIMEON P., JR., 1868–1900
OCTAVIA, 1832–1902
SIMEON P., 1816–1891
EDITH JEWELL, 1888–1954
FRANK LEON, 1869–1934
TIBBETTS, ALBERT E. 13 AUG 1865–2 JAN 1943
CARRIE B. MCKENNEY, WIFE OF ALBERT E. TIBBETTS, 2 APRIL 1864–10 JUNE 1932

On the 1860 census, Simeon P. McKenney was thirty-seven years old and living in Biddeford, where he was an attorney. He and his wife, Octavia, had two children at that time: Nellie, one, and an as-yet-unnamed female infant who was three months old. In 1870, four children were living at home: Clara, ten (who must have been the unnamed baby); Carlos, who was born on September 10, 1864; Simeon Jr., three; and Frank, one. Nellie had most likely died. By 1880, Simeon was operating McKenney and Heard hardware store at 169 Main Street. The family lived at 240 Main Street in Biddeford.

When Carlos reached adulthood, he took over the hardware store and operated it for the rest of his life. He married Elizabeth Nichols, a daughter of Canadian immigrants, who'd been working as a clerk in Biddeford. Carlos's brother Frank married Edith Jewell. Carrie B. McKenney presents a slight mystery. If she's the daughter of Simeon and Octavia, then perhaps she's actually Clara, whose age on the 1880 census was listed as nineteen, more or less confirming her approximate birthdate of 1860. Perhaps she creatively reduced her age a bit (giving herself a new birth year of 1864) when she met Albert, who was born in 1864. It's interesting that Carlos appears to have been the one who purchased the expensive mausoleum. Was it his choice that his are the only life dates *not* included in the plot?

Near their graves is a notable tree. Sometime in about 1845, the groundskeeper of Camperdown House, the ancestral home of the Earl of Camperdown in Scotland, was walking through the forest on the grounds when he came upon a very short tree that had elm-type leaves. He and the Earl agreed that the tree was unlike anything they'd ever seen before and decided to move it into the park area of the grounds. The tree, now known as the Camperdown Elm, survived the move and thrived in the new setting. It turned out that it couldn't reproduce from seeds, but cuttings taken from its drooping branches could be grafted onto rootstock from other trees and would grow into clones of the mother plant. All Camperdown Elms *in the world* are cuttings from the original or its genetically identical daughter trees! Camperdown Elms can be infected with Dutch elm disease, which killed nearly all of America's once stunningly beautiful urban shade trees, but because the Camperdown is so short, the elm bark beetle that spreads the fungus often overlooks this tree, sparing it. Laurel Hill's Camperdown Elm is located about fifty feet to the right of the McKenney plot. On the same corner is a honey locust tree, easily identified by its compound leaves. Honey locusts that haven't been hybridized have long thorns. Legend has it that these thorns were used as pins in the South during the Civil War, as the metal to manufacture pins was all going to the war effort. That tale has resulted in the honey locust also being called the "Confederate Pin Tree."

MARSHALL, MEHITABLE, D, 12 OCT 1852, AGED 75 YRS. 6 MOS.
"AFFLICTION SOME LONG TIME SHE BORE,
PHYSICIANS WERE IN VAIN,
TILL GOD DID PLEASE TO GIVE HER EASE
AND FREE HER FROM HER PAIN."
GORDON, PIKE, D. JULY 1802 AGED 30 YRS. 6 MOS.
GORDON, PIKE, JR., DROWNED 7 AUG 1823 AGED 22 YRS.
HIGGINS, MEHITABLE, D. 29 JAN 1859, AGED 62 YRS.
STORER, SETH S., D. 13 JUNE 1842, AGED 29 YRS.
BROWN, SUSAN A., WIFE OF BENJAMIN F. BROWN, DROWNED 4 SEP 1813, AGED 23 YRS.

Mehitable Goodwin of Biddeford married Pike Gordon on November 5, 1796. He'd been born in 1772, the son of Amos and Mary Gordon. She and Pike had three children: Mehitable, born in May 1797; Susanna ("Susan"); and Pike Jr., born on February 15, 1801. In 1808, Mehitable, now a widow, married for a second time, to Samuel Marshall, and she gave birth to sons Samuel (in 1809), Henry (in 1810) and Isaac (in 1814). In April 1813, her daughter, Mehitable 2nd, who was just sixteen, also gave birth to a child, Seth Storer. No father is listed for Seth in Biddeford's vital records, but Seth Storer, Esq., had recently married and was living in Biddeford. He and his wife would have their first child the same year that Mehitable's illegitimate son was born. If Seth was the father, he was aged twenty-seven to her sixteen. Biddeford midwives probably followed the typical New England custom, so young Mehitable would have been closely questioned when she was in active labor regarding the identity of her baby's father. It was believed that at that point she would almost certainly be truthful, and then the town could use that information to make sure the child's father, instead of taxpayers, provided financial support for his offspring.

In 1815, Mehitable 2nd married Thomas Mores; she later married a second time. In 1850, both Mehitables, mother and daughter, were living with Isaac in Biddeford. How Pike Jr. and Mehitable's granddaughter, the young wife of Benjamin Brown, both drowned (Susan in 1843, not 1813) isn't known, but the Saco River was a strong presence in the lives of nineteenth-century Saco and Biddeford citizens and drownings weren't unusual. Incidentally, at Laurel Hill Cemetery, drowning seems to be the only cause of death that's noted on gravestones.

The shared stone of the two Gordon Pikes has much in common with the gravestones of Thomas Low and his daughter and was likely carved in the same shop—that of Timothy Eastman. The shaping of the tops of these stones is especially artful and challenging to accomplish.

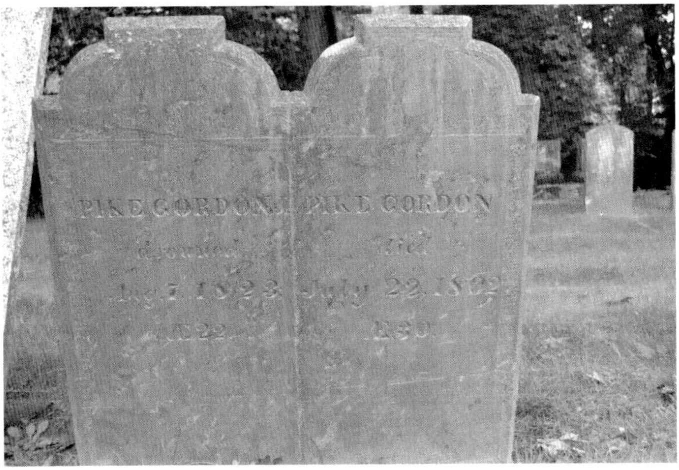

The resting place of Gordon Pike and his son. The top of this stone would have been challenging to cut. *Authors' collection.*

RICE, FRANCIS WARREN, BUXTON, ME., 1 JAN 1815–SACO, ME., 22 SEPT 1888
"AS A MODEL HUSBAND AND FATHER HIS BEREFT WIFE AND CHILDREN LOVINGLY REMEMBER HIM."
RICHARD W., SON OF FRANCIS W. RICE, 23 JUNE 1862–9 MAY 1940
EMMA C., WIFE OF RICHARD W. RICE, 3 OCT 1864–

Frances Warren Rice was born in Buxton in 1815. On the 1870 census, he was listed as having no occupation, but he had an estate valued at $10,000, very large for the time. His wife, Carmine, and their six children were all born in New Granada (a country that was later divided into Colombia, Ecuador, Venezuela and Panama). Rice had started his career as a newspaperman, writing first for the *Maine Palladium* and then a newspaper in Boston called the *Olive Branch*; finally, after relocating to San Francisco, he founded and wrote for the *Courier*. In the mid-1800s, he served as the U.S. consul to Mexico and New Granada, which is where he must have met Carmine. The Rice plot is dominated by an immense sculpture of an angel.

Behind the Rice family plot is a truly massive Norway spruce that also appears as a mature tree in a postcard image that's dated 1906. Given the tree's immense size, it's possible that this spruce dates from the original founding of the cemetery. In fact, it may be the only remaining tree from that time.

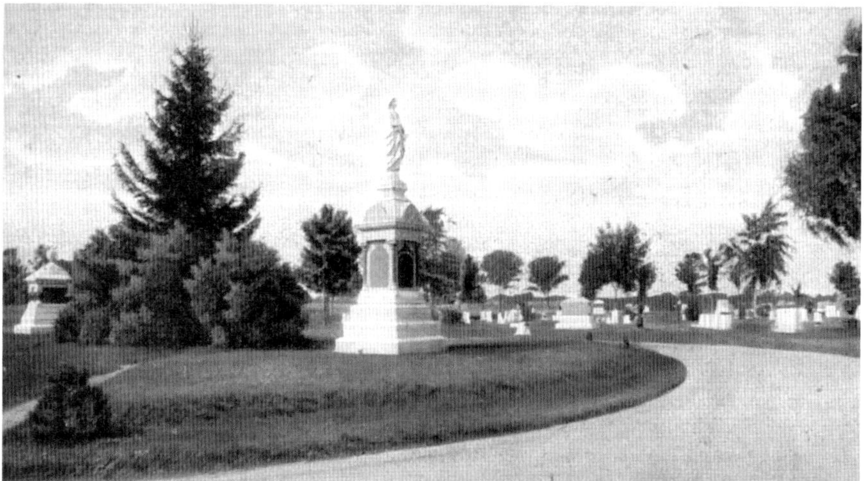

A postcard view from about 1910 of the Francis Rice plot. *Collection of Dyer Library/Saco Museum.*

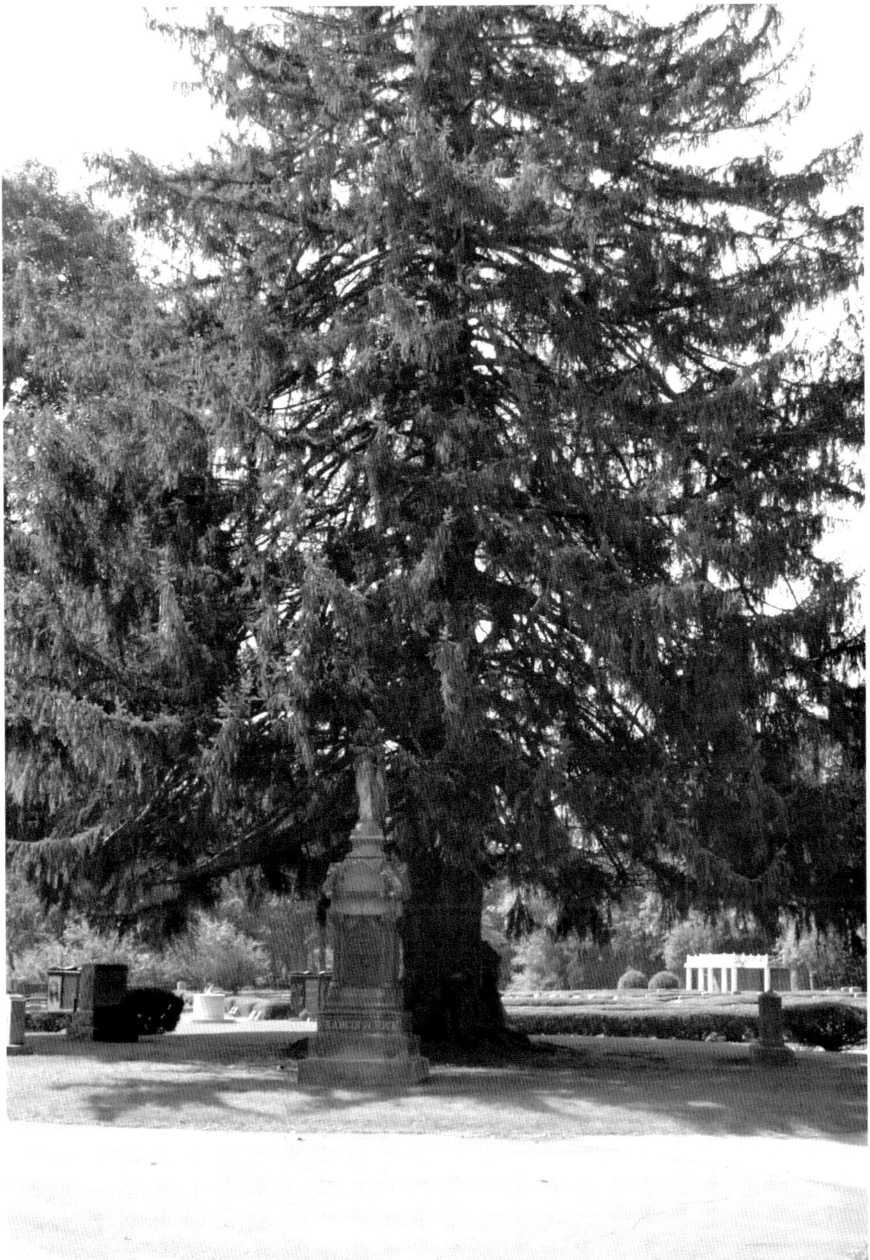

The same scene in 2017, with the Norway spruce dwarfing the angel. *Authors' collection.*

THE LOWER AREA AND LOWER WEST AVENUE

Luce, Rev. Israel, 21 Nov 1834–28 Dec 1908
Alice E., 1839–1928
Gilbert Haven, 9 March 1879–11 Feb 1902
Magdalene, 16 Nov 1807–16 June 1886
McGulloch, Dr. L., 3 March 1810–3 Dec 1894
Catharine, wife of Dr. L. McGulloch 19 Sept 1813–2 May 1898

Although all of Laurel Hill Cemetery is lovely, there are surely some sections that are more attractive than others. The site where several members of Methodist minister Israel Luce's family are buried has a grand view of the Saco River, but it's located on a level below the rest of the cemetery. A paved road once provided access, but it long ago reverted to grass. Farther along this lower level is the ravine side, where many paupers are interred—some with markers but many without—and even deeper into the forest are the graves of many babies, most marked just with concrete numbers.

In life, Israel put his calling above the desire for money; he was never well paid. Born in New York, he was expected to travel, like most Methodist ministers. Several of his children were born in Vermont; others came after he was transferred to Maine. In 1870, he was living in Portland. By 1880, his ministry took him to Lewiston. In 1888, he was named in the Biddeford City Directory, having a summer residence in "Gookin field." Then he was back in Portland, where he was the assistant pastor of the Chestnut Street Methodist Church in the late 1890s. Finally, he was sent to Berwick, his last parish. He and Alice E. Oastrum, the McGullochs' daughter, had at least eight children. Paul, Israel and Gilbert are all buried nearby. Gilbert was still a student when he died of kidney failure at the age of twenty-three. Their son Frederick probably also died young, appearing as a seven-year-old on the 1870 census but not on the 1880. Perhaps it was while he was summering with his family in Biddeford that Israel became familiar with Laurel Hill and chose this quiet resting place for his family.

HOOPER, SYLVESTER, 1847–1919
SARAH P., 1850–1916
MARY H., 1852–1922
SAMUEL, 1805–1886
DORCUS, WIFE OF SAMUEL HOOPER, 1810–1905
ALBERT, 1836–1884
CALEB S., 1837–1862, D. AT SHIP ISLAND, MISSISSIPPI
ORLANDO, 1842–1862, D. AT SHIP ISLAND, MISSISSIPPI
SAMUEL, 1843–1870, D. AT JACKSON, MICHIGAN

Samuel Hooper was the son of George Hooper and Sarah Tarbox, who farmed in Biddeford. In his younger years, Samuel was never a financial success, often employed just as a laborer, but later in life he acquired a farm in Saco and did better. He first married Martha Tarbox, who died in 1830 less than two years after their son, George, was born. Samuel then married Dorcus Staples. The couple was very prolific. Their children were Albert (1836), Caleb (1837), Martha (1839), Ambrose (1840), Orlando (1842), Samuel (1843), Sumner (1845), Silvester (1846), Arthur (1849), Helen (1850) and Mary (1852). On December 1, 1861, Caleb, Orlando and Samuel Jr. enlisted in Company K of the Thirteenth Maine Volunteers. In February, the Thirteenth was sent south on an arduous, storm-wracked voyage to a tiny island off the coast of Mississippi named Ship Island. The isle had bad water, poor food, desperate sanitary conditions and rampant disease, especially dysentery. Caleb was afflicted first and died in the company hospital on June 19, 1862. His younger brother only survived another few weeks, dying on July 2, 1862. Of the 236 men of the Thirteenth who died during service, only 22 died of wounds; the rest were killed by disease. For all soldiers who died during the Civil War, about 62 percent succumbed to disease rather than battle. For the Thirteenth, about 90 percent of the fatalities were due to disease—probably a reflection of where the Thirteenth spent most of the war, in places like Ship Island.

Sylvester married Sarah Paget of Biddeford and spent the rest of his life as a clergyman in various Maine towns. They had no children. Helen and Mary never married. Mary taught school for a time, and Helen helped manage the farm that she ran alone in the last years of her life. Albert never married and worked on his father's farm until his death. Samuel Jr. served for the entire Civil War and was promoted to corporal. His younger brother Arthur spent some time in Jackson, Michigan, returned to Maine and then went back to Michigan, where his wife divorced him for desertion and non-support in 1917. Samuel may have been there visiting when he died in Jackson in 1870 of typhoid fever.

Although the Hooper family plot is marked with a modern gravestone, it's located in the paupers' section of the cemetery. It can be reached by walking into the woods at the far end of River Avenue (well past the Luce plot) or can be viewed by looking into the ravine when standing to the left rear of the Cornelius Sweetser family plot. The number of poor people who were buried in the cemetery in unmarked graves is unknown.

DEERING, JOSEPH, SON OF JOSEPH G. AND JOSEPHINE DEERING, D. 20 JULY 1879, AGED 10 YRS.

JOSEPHINE NEALLY, B. SOUTH BERWICK, 25 FEB 1844, D. SACO, 20 NOV 1928

JOSEPH GODFREY, B. WATERBORO, 7 SEPT 1816, D. SACO, 29 FEB 1892

ANNIE GRAY WIGGIN, WIFE OF FRANK G. DEERING, 3 FEB 1864–7 MARCH 1895

LOVE, GEORGE RUSK, 1868–1946

HELEN JOSEPHINE DEERING, 1880–

DEERING, MARY H. CUTTER, WIFE OF JOSEPH G. DEERING, D. 6 NOV 1858, AGED 29 YRS.

DEERING, FRANK CUTTER, 28 JAN 1866–12 AUG 1939.

"A DETERMINED WORKER, LOYAL TO HIS FRIENDS, A DEVOTED STUDENT OF THE CULTURAL ARTS, EVER SEEKING TO IMPROVE AND BEAUTIFY THIS COMMUNITY IN WHICH HE LIVED."

FANNY CHASE, 8 APR 1872–31 MAY 1947

On the 1860 census, merchant Joseph Godfrey Deering was living with two tenants. His personal estate was valued at an impressive $20,000, with another $9,000 in real estate. His first wife, Mary Cutter, had died two years before, aged just twenty-nine. Even wealth didn't protect against rampant disease. By 1870, he'd married Josephine Neally, who was twenty-six to his fifty-three, and his total value was up to $100,000. They had two children at home: Frank, who was four, and Joseph G. Jr., just four months old and who would only live to the age of ten. Joseph Sr. was listed as a retired grocer. Josephine was described as "disabled from childbirth." By the time of the 1880 census, Joseph Sr. had gone back to work—now as a lumber dealer—and Josephine was pregnant with their daughter, Helen Josephine, who'd be born later that year (she'd eventually marry an Ohio-born physician, George R. Love, and live with him and their only child, George, in Toledo, Ohio, for many years before returning to Saco). The Deerings had a live-in Irish servant, Maggie Kelly, who, at sixteen, was just two years older than Frank. They had a partially finished attic space in their Main Street mansion that was perfect for housing a servant, and they nearly always had one living in.

Joseph Sr. died in 1892, leaving the management of his various financial interests to his son, Frank. Frank Cutter Deering married Annie Gray Wiggin in 1890, but she died just five years later at thirty-one. They had two children: Annie Katherine, born in 1892, and Joseph Godfrey, born two years later. In early 1900, Frank married Frances Chase ("Fanny"), and they both profited from the family's continued lumber business (Frank could have been justly called a "lumber baron" by this point). Frank's mother, Josephine, continued to live with him until her death in 1928. Frank Cutter Deering joined the board of trustees of the Dyer Library in 1907, eventually replaced by his son, Joseph "Joe" Deering.

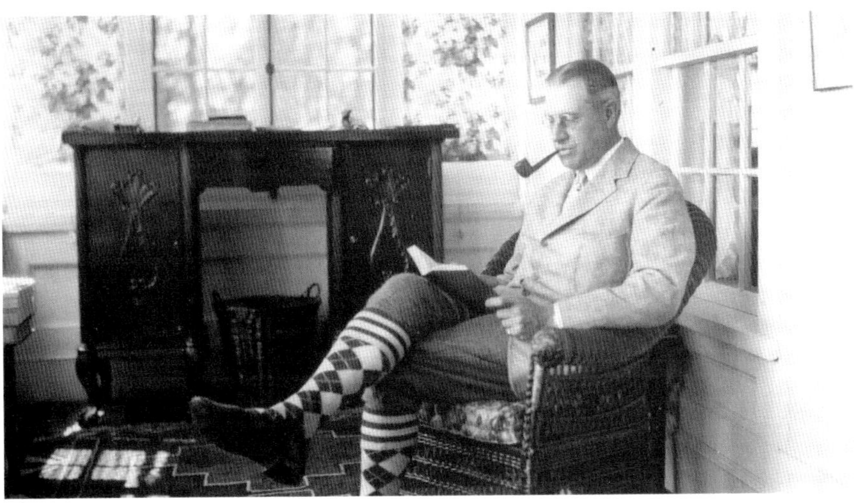

Frank Cutter Deering in natty attire. *Collection of Dyer Library/Saco Museum.*

In 1955, "Miss Katherine" (as she was known) and Joe gave their family home at 371 Main Street to the Dyer Library. Joe remained a very active member of the board almost up to the time of his death. Joe Deering and his wife, Elise Dabney, had two daughters. In 1956, the city directory listed him as "President of J.G. Deering and Son Lumber Co., the Saco River Driving Co., the York National Bank, the Mutual Insurance Co., and the Inn at Biddeford Pool." He died in 1987.

LOWE, NATHANIEL M., 4.29.1925, LIVED 84 YRS.
JANE, WIFE OF N.M. LOWE, X, VIII, 1865–IV, III, 1827

Nathaniel was a maker of pianofortes. He's buried with his first wife, Jane, whom he outlived by forty-four years, although he may have married twice more—the last time when he was eighty-one. It's very unusual that Jane's dates of birth and death are given in Roman numerals. Perhaps the use of Roman numerals, as well as the design of his strange gravestone-within-a-gravestone, had meaning at the time, but if so, it has been lost now.

HIGHT, ELLEN MARIA, DAU. OF ELISHA AND ELIZABETH HIGHT, 11 SEPT 1830–27 FEB 1919
MYRA CHASE, DAU. OF ELISHA AND ELIZABETH HIGHT, 28 JULY 1837–2 OCT 1917
E. FRANKLIN, 26 JAN 1829–14 MAY 1891
ELISHA, D. 29 DEC 1881 AGED 76 YRS.
ELIZABETH H., WIFE OF ELISHA HIGHT, 7 JULY 1806–18 DEC 1888
MERRILL, FRANCES E., D. 21 SEPT 1913
MASON, MABEL, 18 NOV 1859–28 OCT 1924
LUTHER T., 16 FEB 1834–20 AUG 1907
SUSAN C., 19 JUNE 1843–20 OCT 1921
LIZZIE HIGHT, WIFE OF LUTHER T. MASON, 4 AUG 1835–7 SEPT 1865

Sometime in 1828, Elizabeth Hannaford, the daughter of Zaccheus Hannaford and Betsy Simonton of Portland, and her fiancé, Elisha Hight, sat for their portraits, done by local artist William S. Gookin. Elizabeth swept her dark-brown hair up and fastened it in place with a large comb. The dress she chose was light-brown silk with a delicate lace inset in the scoop neckline. Her massive sleeves, set low on her arms, helped to enhance the V-shape from neck to elbow (almost seeming to have no shoulders at all) that was the current style. She wore a long black necklace, looped twice around her slender neck. Elisha wore a shawl-collared coat with a black tie, with the collar turned stiffly up on his shirt. The dark coat contrasted nicely with his blue eyes.

After the couple exchanged vows, babies were the next order of business. Three boys and six girls would follow in rapid succession, the last born in 1849. Elisha operated a livery stable but later worked in the cotton mill and then as a harness maker. The family took up residence on Middle Street. Their third daughter, Sarah Elizabeth, married Biddeford attorney Luther Mason. She gave birth to Mabel, who never married, and Frederick before her early death. Luther was living in a rooming house (with Richmond Ingersoll, among many others) in 1870. He'd placed young Frederick with his father-in-law, but where Mabel was living is unknown. By 1880, the three resided together again, just shortly before Luther remarried to Susan C. Smith. Ellen Hight never married, living out her life in the family home. She died there of pneumonia at the age of eighty-eight. The Hights' daughter Almira ("Myra") also never married; she worked as a housekeeper and died in Biddeford at the age of eighty. Frances ("Fannie") married John P. Merrill. On the 1880 census, he was working in a livery stable in Bangor, and she was employed as a "painter of pictures." By 1900, he'd died and she'd moved back to Saco, where she supported herself for the rest of her life by giving art lessons, dying of acute nephritis at the age of seventy.

The Hights' son Henry served for almost the entire Civil War, achieving an impressive rise from private to captain. He married Lucy Mason and moved to the Boston area, where he worked as a clerk in a store. He named his eldest daughter, Sarah Elizabeth, after his deceased older sister. He died in 1911 and is also buried at Laurel Hill Cemetery. Octavius Hight served in the Civil War as a substitute (in place of a person who'd been drafted but paid someone else to serve instead) and eventually settled in Butte, Montana, and then San Diego, California, living on until after 1930. He married twice but had no children. The portraits of Elisha and Elizabeth remained in the family, passed from one generation to the next, until 2017.

WEST AVENUE FROM SOUTH TO NORTH

Cleaves, Daniel, d. 9 Dec 1817, aged 47 yrs.
Sarah, wife of Daniel Cleaves, d. May 1835, aged 65 yrs.
Daniel, d. 1 July 1865, aged 56 yrs.
Marcia Tucker, wife of Daniel Cleaves, 7 Sept 1816–4 May 1886
Mary, 24 May 1803–13 Sept 1871
William, son of Daniel and Sarah Cleaves, d. 30 June 1801, aged 3 yrs.
John, son of Daniel and Sarah Cleaves, d. 5 July 1802, aged 2 yrs.
Abigail, dau. of Daniel and Sarah Cleaves, d. 16 July 1802, aged 6 yrs.
Dummer, Charles, 3 Sept 1793–28 June 1872
Almira C., 19 Sept 1806–25 Sept 1886
Fairfield, John, 1736–1819
Mary G., wife of John Fairfield, 1737–1774
Elizabeth, wife of John Fairfield, 1760–1841

Daniel Cleaves was born in Danvers, Massachusetts, the son of Putnam Cleaves and Abigail Jacobs. He came to Saco in about 1790 and went into business. A brief biography claims that he was among the most successful of merchants in York County. At the time of his death, he possessed a sizable estate that included ten other homes and farms, besides his own, that he rented out, as well as expansive tracts of land. He married Sarah, a daughter of longtime Saco minister Reverend John Fairfield. Daniel Cleaves Jr., son of Daniel and Sarah Cleaves, was also a very well-to-do merchant in Saco. He was born not long after his parents had suffered through the deaths of three of their young children: three-year-old William in 1801, followed by two-year-old John and six-year-old Abigail just two weeks apart in 1802.

Daniel married Hannah Marcia Tucker, the daughter of his father's sixteen-year mercantile partner, Jonathan Tucker, in 1835. Daniel and Marcia would have four children of their own, although their first daughter, Sarah, died at birth. The Saco Museum owns a fabulous portrait that's said to be of Marcia with her infant daughter, also named Marcia, who was born in 1838.

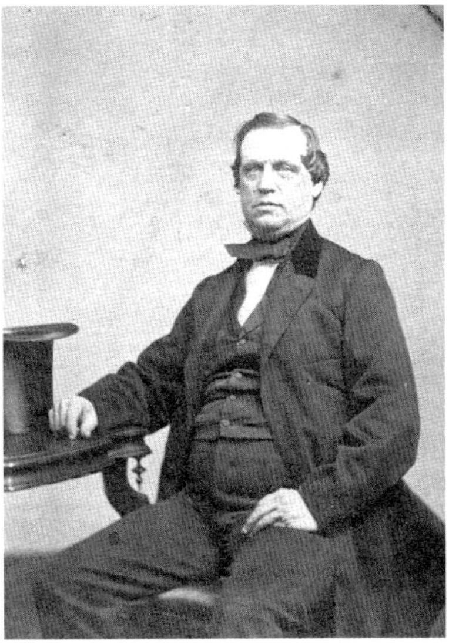

Daniel Cleaves Jr., photographed very shortly before his death. *Collection of Dyer Library/Saco Museum.*

Almira, who married John Dummer, was also one of Daniel Sr. and Sarah Cleaves's children. In the Saco Museum collection is a receipt for the removal of ten bodies from the Cleaves tomb in Biddeford, their burial in Laurel Hill and the purchase of a monument ($773.00) from Oliver Wentworth, who was a Boston marble dealer, as well as for granite work by Woodbury G. Gooch (who ran a granite and tombstone business in Biddeford), an additional $910.00—a total equivalent to about $28,000 in 2017.

Reverend John Fairfield was an important person in Saco history. He was born in Boston, Massachusetts, the son of William Fairfield and Elizabeth White and attended Harvard College. He first came to Saco in 1761 to preach at First Parish Church in what was a sort of audition to see if members of the parish would like both his style of preaching and the quality of the man. It seems that they did. He was called to be their minister and ordained in 1762, the same year that he married Mary Goodwin in Berwick, Maine. Mary was the mother of all five of his children: Ichabod, Elizabeth, Mary, Sally and Hannah. Ichabod's son John served as a governor of Maine. After his wife died, Reverend John married Martha Ruggles. He held the post at First Parish until 1799; then, being an elderly man (for the time) at age sixty-two, he retired to Massachusetts.

For nearly all of that time, he kept a terse diary that's served as the lone source on many births, deaths and marriages in the area. One of the deaths he noted was that of his own grandson on July 7, 1801. Reverend John reported that he had had a visitor: "He informs me that my grandchild

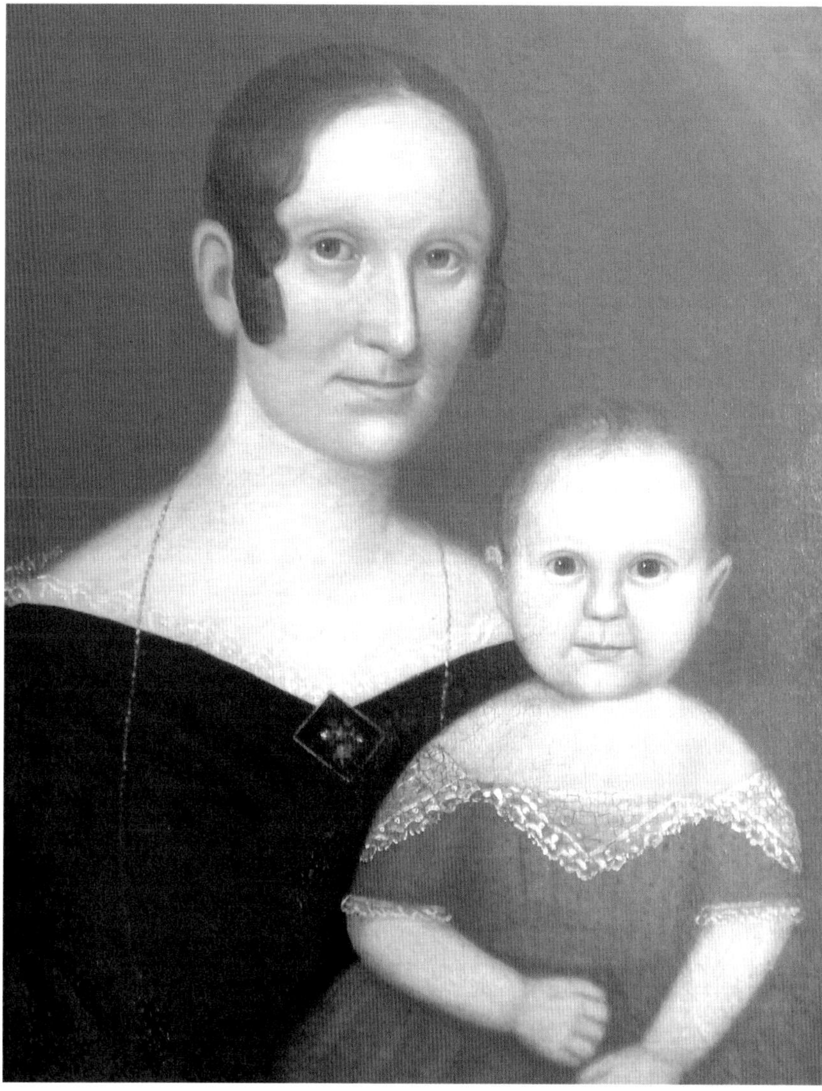

Hannah Marcia Cleaves and her first surviving child, Marcia, circa 1838. *Collection of Saco Museum.*

Wm Cleaves about 4 years old fell from his father's wharf in Saco into the river & was drowned, tho perhaps taken out alive on Tuesday last but died immediately & was buried the next day." John is buried with two of his three wives: Mary and Elizabeth Sweetser, whom he married in 1809. Martha Ruggles is buried elsewhere.

Tucker, Jonathan, [Father], 13 March 1776–9 Feb 1861
Hannah S. [Mother], wife of Jonathan Tucker, 21 Apr 1781–27 Jan 1858
McArthur, Almira Locke, 1871–1950
Locke, John S., 1836–1906
Marcia C., 1838–1914

Jonathan Tucker was born in 1776 in Salem, Massachusetts. By 1800, he'd relocated to Saco, where he ran a successful store, and married Hannah Scamman, the daughter of Nathaniel and Sarah Jordan Scamman. They were the parents of four sons, followed by four daughters. The second youngest of those was Hannah Marcia Tucker, who married Daniel Cleaves. The Cleaves had four children. Their daughter Marcia, born in 1838, married John S. Locke (born in Biddeford but working as a "stationer" in Boston at the time of their marriage). The Lockes remained in Boston (amassing a considerable fortune), where their only child, Almira, was born in 1871. Just before 1880, they returned to Saco and moved into their home on Middle Street. Later, John became the superintendent of schools for Saco; Locke School was named for him. He was deeply involved in the York Institute in its early years.

Almira grew up in comfort and wealth. In 1895, she married George Wood McArthur, who also grew up wealthy. His father, an immigrant, began his working career as a child, laboring as a bobbin boy in a Rhode Island mill. Through thrift and hard work, he advanced rapidly, and by the time George was entering his teen years, his father was well-off. Born in New Jersey, George was prep school–educated and graduated from Bowdoin College. After briefly working as the principal of Wells High School, he resigned due to poor health. He traveled in the South but then settled in a large home on Adams Street in Biddeford and took up work as the assistant superintendent of the Pepperell Mill, where his father had been longtime overseer. By 1910, George had retired. The census described his financial situation as "own income," but he was also in poor health. He died in Biddeford at the age of forty-four in 1916 of a cerebral hemorrhage after "many years of ill health." George was buried in Woonsocket, Rhode Island, where his father was already interred.

After George's death, Almira moved back to the family home on Middle Street. In 1915, she paid $580 to George E. Morrison & Son of Portland for the large granite monument and the two smaller markers for Marcia and John. Morrison described the work on the receipt as "a first class job in every detail" and went on to say that his company was "very much pleased with this

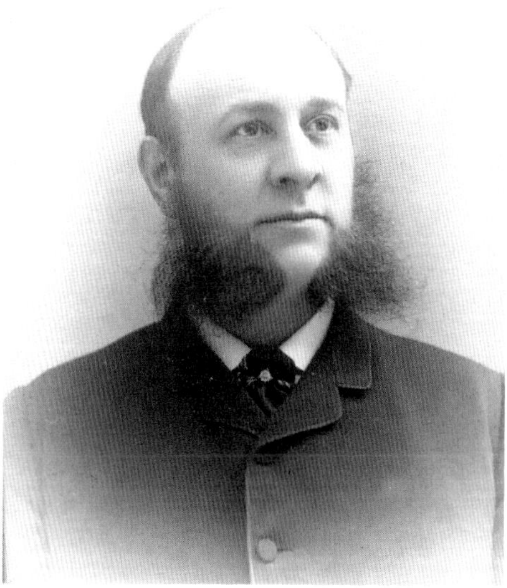

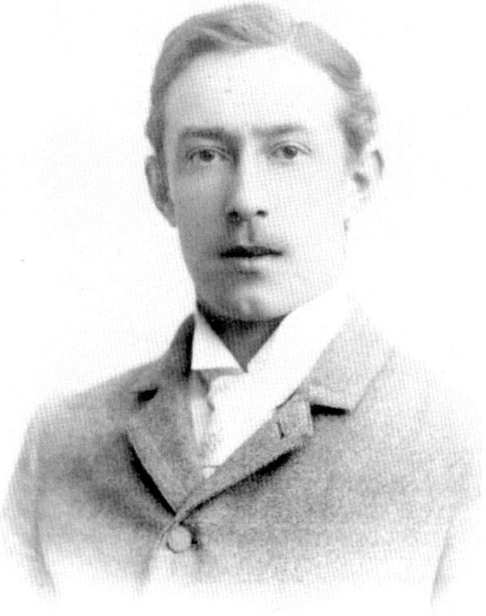

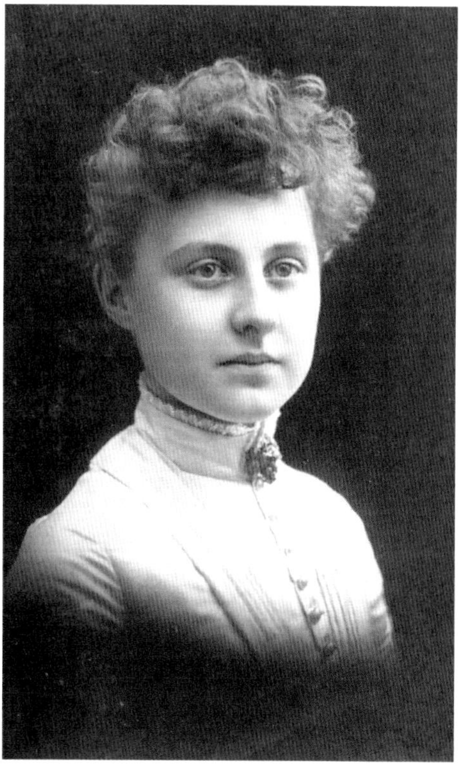

Above, left: John S. Locke in about 1870, proudly sporting impressive sideburns. *Collection of Dyer Library/Saco Museum.*

Above, right: George Wood McArthur spent much of his adult life in poor health. *Collection of Dyer Library/Saco Museum.*

Left: Almira Locke's 1888 graduation photo from Saco High School. *Collection of Dyer Library/Saco Museum.*

monument as it certainly is a very nice piece of work"—perhaps reassuring Almira in case she might not find it so satisfying? When the United States entered World War I in 1917, she became a very active volunteer in the Red Cross, a role she continued after the war ended. She traveled extensively and remained involved in civic work for the rest of her life. She never remarried and lived alone for many years. She bequeathed many of her family pieces to the York Institute, continuing her father's interest in the museum.

WEBBER, JAMES M. B. 1880–1962
BERTHA M. STAPLES, WIFE OF JAMES M. B. WEBBER, 1877–1960
CHARLES HORACE, 16 JULY 1831–30 JULY 1899
EMMA BURBANK, WIFE OF CHARLES H. WEBBER, 26 JULY 1852–12 JUNE 1926
WENDEL PHILLIPS, SON OF C. H. AND EMMA B. WEBBER, 16 JUNE 1891–11 JULY 1891
BURBANK, CHARLES EDWIN, ONLY SON OF JAMES M. AND PHEBE H. BURBANK, 26 OCT 1855, AGED 18 YRS. 8 MOS. 8 DAYS
JAMES M., D. 26 APR 1875, AGED 63 YRS. 4 MOS.
PHEBE H., 14 FEB 1811–7 DEC 1902

James, Phebe and Charles Burbank are buried with the Webber family, into which James's sister, Emma, married. The Honorable James M. Burbank was born in Newfield, Maine. He moved to Waterboro, Maine, in young adulthood, working as a merchant. Next he served as the postmaster and then completed a term in the state legislature. In about 1846, he moved to Springvale and opened a hotel but remained very active in the Democratic Party, holding various local positions. Sometime after his son's death in 1855, James moved his family to Saco, where he served as the high sheriff of York County and then as a state senator. Charles Edwin was the Burbanks' only son and eldest child. *The History of Sanford, Maine* noted that he "was a young man of great promise." Robert P. Berry, who ran a "public house" in Alfred, Maine, and who was also a part-time gravestone carver, chiseled into young Charles's stone, "Weep not for me my kindred dear/I am not dead but slumber here/ Dry up your tears they're all in vain/We only part to meet again."

The Burbanks also had three daughters: Emma, Ellen and Ann. When Emma married Charles Horace Webber, he acquired not just a wife but also possession of the Burbank family home. Born in Stoneham, Massachusetts, Charles was the son of a minister. In 1851, he married Susan Adams Huckins. The couple had two sons. In 1872, Charles and Susan separated when he assumed the pastorate of the Cutts Street Baptist Church, one of two Baptist congregations in Saco at the time. The younger son remained with Susan; the elder moved to Saco. In 1877, Charles left the ministry (perhaps forced out because of his then-scandalous divorce from Susan) and afterward ran a men's clothing and hat store on Main Street for several years. After his second marriage, Charles moved in with his new bride and her mother. John Haley—local historian and something of a town gossip—didn't especially like Charles and described him as "the Rev. quack of unhappy memory." Whatever caused Haley to recall Charles's unpleasant reputation (besides his un-reverend-like marital behavior) is now forgotten. At the time of their marriage in 1880, Charles was forty-eight and Emma only twenty-seven, having been born the year after Charles's first marriage. Wendel, who died as a newborn, was their second son; three others lived to adulthood, including James M.B. Webber. Charles died of angina in Old Orchard Beach.

Rounds, Oscar W. 1851–1916
Julia A. wife of Oscar W. Rounds, 1855–1931
Clyde, son of Oscar W. and Julia A. Rounds, d. 11 Apr 1885, aged 1 year 9 mos.
Gertie M., only child of Oscar W. and Julia A. Rounds, aged 4 yrs. 8 mos.
Bean, John, d. 3 Sept 1880, aged 48 yrs. 5 mos.
Mary E., wife of John Bean, d. 1 March 1906, aged 76 yrs. 11 mos.

Oscar Rounds was the son of Daniel and Elizabeth Rounds. His father worked variously in the mills as a "headmaker" or sometimes as a lumberman. Oscar worked first as a heading maker as well, sometimes as a box maker and at times for the railroad. Oscar married Julia A. Bean, and they had three children: Gertie, who was probably born after the 1870 census but who had already died by 1880; Clyde, who was born and died between federal censuses and thus also missed being enumerated; and Daniel, born in 1882, who lived into adulthood. The Rounds family always lived at 71 Bradley Street in Saco. Carved into Clyde's gravestone is, "Our little boy/Too fair for earth." Gertie's reads, "She sailed from our vision/Like a calm, sweet summer day."

Small monuments like these are spread throughout Laurel Hill and almost always mark the graves of very young children. Although it's impossible to come up with an absolutely accurate figure because of a lack of recordkeeping, during the nineteenth century about 20 percent of children died before their first birthday and more than 30 percent by their fifth. Around the beginning of the twentieth century, those numbers began to show a very slow, gradual improvement. Carved into Gertie's little stone is the name of the carver, O.L. Allen. Oliver L. Allen was twenty-nine when he was named on the 1870 census. Born in New Hampshire, this marble worker lived in Biddeford, first as a boarder, but by 1880 he was married and the father of two young children and owned a home. Living with him in 1880 was his younger brother, William, who was also a marble worker.

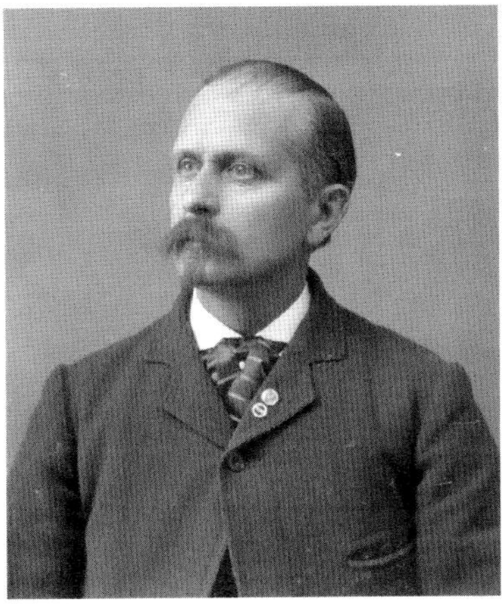

Oscar Rounds donned his Sunday best for his photograph. *Collection of Dyer Library/Saco Museum.*

FAIRFIELD, JOSIAH, ESQ., "WHO WAS RESPECTED AND USEFUL, AS A MAN A PHYSICIAN AND A MAGISTRATE," D. 23 JUNE 1794, AGED 47 YRS.
THORNTON, RICHARD CUTTS, 27 MAY 1797–26 AUG 1873
LYDIA H. GILMAN, 20 MAY 1799–19 JUNE 1886

Josiah Fairfield is buried under a gravestone with a design that was typical of the late eighteenth century but would hardly be used at all afterward. Unlike earlier versions, the death's head or winged cherub seems quite placid, if not just a bit cheerful. It certainly doesn't display the grim realism that earlier skeletal ones did. The unusual lettering on his stone was quite likely carved by Caleb Lamson 2nd, one of a long line of Lamson family carvers in Charlestown, Massachusetts. According to George Folsom, who wrote a history of Biddeford and Saco in 1830, Josiah, a cousin of Reverend John Fairfield, came to Pepperrellborough in about 1770. Although he initially practiced medicine (which may have been a great relief to the unfortunate Dr. Aaron Porter, who had been the only practicing physician for a vast area that included Biddeford, Kennebunk and Alfred), Fairfield quickly gave that up to begin a more lucrative business career.

He spent the Revolutionary War years fitting out privateers, as well as serving as a magistrate. The engraving on his gravestone makes it clear that he was well liked. He died of consumption and was originally buried in the Pepperrell burying ground. How his gravestone came to be placed later in the plot of Richard Cutts Thornton (or vice versa), who died many years later, is unclear.

Richard was the third child of Sarah "Sally" Cutts and Thomas Gilbert Thornton. Like his surviving siblings, he attended Thornton Academy. Richard became a farmer of middling success and lived for many years on Cross Street. In 1850, he had sixty "unimproved" acres and another forty that were improved, on which he grew Indian corn—a popular crop among his neighbors. He also owned two horses, two cows, a team of oxen, a small flock of sheep and a pig. Richard married Lydia Gilman. Lydia's parents couldn't be determined; she appears not to have been born in the Biddeford/Saco area. On the 1840 census, there's a young woman in their household, aged fifteen to nineteen. She could be a daughter or perhaps hired help. A published Cutts family genealogy erroneously reported that Richard died young.

BERRY, JOHN ADAMS, M.D., 1808–1879
OLIVIA DONNELL, WIFE OF JOHN ADAMS BERRY, M.D., 1814–1896
DENNETT, J. VAUGHAN, 1867–1959
ELLEN BOWERS, WIFE OF J. VAUGHAN DENNETT, 1869–1953
DOROTHY, DAU. OF J. VAUGHAN AND ELLEN BOWERS DENNETT, 1901–1980
ROSCOE G., M.D. D. 3 JULY 1877, AGED 42 YEARS, 4 MOS.
ANNIE O. BERRY, WIFE OF ROSCOE G. DENNETT, M.D., D. 29 FEB 1924, AGED 85 YEARS, 10 DAYS
BESSIE G., DAU. OF ROSCOE G. AND ANNIE O. DENNETT, 1875–1878
OLIVIA, DAU. OF J.V. AND E.B. DENNETT, 1896–1897
ELLIOT V., SON OF J.V. AND E.B. DENNETT, 1898–1925
BARBARA, DAU. OF J. V. AND E.B. DENNETT, 1901–1909
BOWERS, ANNIE G., 12 MAY 1864–18 JAN 1925
WALTER T., 27 NOV 1862-1 JULY 1928
SARAH ABBIE BERRY, WIFE OF ROSCOE L. BOWERS, 19 DEC 1837–13 SEPT 1929
ROSCOE L., 18 JAN 1834–6 JULY 1892

James Vaughan Dennett, the son of Roscoe G. Dennett and Annie O. Berry, was born in Saco and grew up there, but by the time of his marriage to Ellen Bowers—the daughter of Roscoe Bowers and Sarah Abbie Berry, his mother's sister—he was living in Massachusetts. Annie and Sarah Abbie

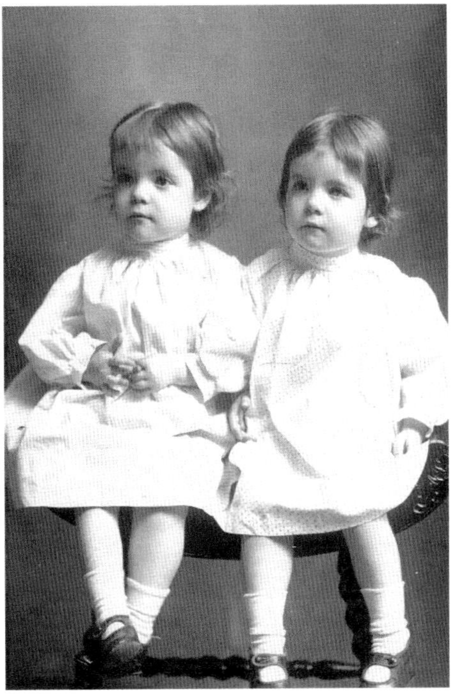

Dennett twins Barbara and Dorothy sat very still for their first photograph. *Collection of Dyer Library/Saco Museum.*

Berry were both the daughters of allopathic physician John Adams Berry and his wife, Olivia Donnell. The great-grandson of a ship's captain, J. Vaughan began his adult life by going to sea, traveling to India as the mate on a sailing ship. After two years, with the age of sail drawing to a close and having no interest in mechanized shipping, he left the sea to attend the Massachusetts Institute of Technology. J. Vaughan lived for the next thirty years in Massachusetts, primarily in Framingham, where he worked in building construction, especially in creating (recently invented) reinforced concrete structures. Of J. Vaughan Dennett's children, only Dorothy lived a long life. She became a nurse.

By 1940, the Dennetts had returned to Saco and were living in a home on Cross Street. J. Vaughan was now retired but kept busy crafting furniture. He seems to have been a man with a strong sense of humor. Many photographs depict him clowning around, often in some kind of costume. He was a major supporter of the York Institute (now Saco Museum) after he moved back to Saco. A mystery, though, is how Roscoe Berry and Roscoe Dennett share the same unusual first name. Before the Berry sisters married into the two families, there doesn't appear to be any connection between them. Perhaps it was that coincidence of the same first name that began a connection.

Burns, Kendrick, [Father], 1889–1955
Mary Nagel [Mother], 1889–1951
Alan L., 1904–1958
Mildred E., 1894–1954
Henry McCauley [Father], 1853–1936
Clementine Kendrick [Mother], 1852–1922
Robert Gordon, 30 Oct 1891–9 Dec 1938
Crossley, Emily Burns, 1883–1965
Kendrick, Humphrey Pike [Father], 1810–1886
Jane Parcher [Mother], 1814–1906
Col. Frank A., "A martyr in the cause of freedom, d. in New Orleans, La., 31 March 1865, aged 30 yrs. 6 mos. 19 days. A tribute to the memory of their Commander by the 61st U.S.C. Infantry"

Clementine Kendrick Burns was born in 1852. Her father, Humphrey Pike Kendrick, was a carpenter but also ran a store in Saco. "H.B. Kendrick & Co." at 254 Main Street sold stationery, books and china but also offered library services for a fee. Items cost two cents per day to check out. Henry Burns, the man she married in 1878, was working in her father's store when she met him. She and Henry had six children: Margaret, Emily, Isabelle, Kendrick, Robert and Alan, born between 1877 and 1894. Eventually, Henry took over the family business (that they were still operating when Clementine died in 1922). They lived for many years on Middle Street. In 1923, construction was completed on a large brick school on Middle Street that was named for Clementine for her "great civic interest."

Colonel Frank A. Kendrick was Clementine's brother. He enlisted as a captain in the Civil War and was eventually promoted to colonel and given command of the First Colored Brigade of the Sixty-First United States Colored Infantry. He was wounded once, quickly returned to service and died of "malarial typhoid fever" in the closing days of the Civil War in New Orleans. Around 185,000 African American men served during the Civil War, but—reflecting biases of the era—nearly all of their officers were white. It seems that his men must have collected money to pay for Colonel Kendrick's lavish and expensive memorial.

MACMILLAN, CHARLES S., 16 AUG 1885–8 JAN 1963
BERTHA LOWELL, 5 JAN 1892–27 OCT 1979
LOWELL, REBA M. 1894–1918
FREDERICK E. [FATHER], 13 MARCH 1856–12 AUG 1930
CLIMENIA P. [MOTHER], 14 FEB 1864–14 AUG 1950
GEORGE S. 6 APR 1826–29 JUNE 1908
LUCY A., WIFE OF GEORGE S. LOWELL, 25 MARCH 1826–15 MARCH 1909
CHARLEY W., SON OF GEORGE S. AND LUCY A. LOWELL, D. 15 AUG 1862, AGED 8 YRS. 6 MOS.
IDA MAY, WIFE OF WILLIAM E. LOWELL, 22 FEB 1853–18 NOV 1884
WILLIAM E., 2 JULY 1858–4 JUNE 1911
GEORGE W., 24 JUNE 1893–6 SEPT. 1938
GEORGE F., JR., 1 JULY 1883–27 JULY 1883
MARY E. REECE, WIFE OF GEORGE F. LOWELL, 6 AUG 1849–2 APR 1888
GREEN, FRANCES M., D. 5 JUNE 1879, AGED 10 YRS. 11 MOS.

The Lowell family plot is a fine example of how the founders of Laurel Hill Cemetery imagined that it would be used. The plot is the final resting place for several generations of this middle-class family, some of whom never lived in Saco, or even in Maine, but who were brought here upon death to be interred with parents, siblings and cousins. George Sutherland Lowell was the great-grandson of a Revolutionary War veteran. He married Lucy Bridges, and they were parents to five children: Charley, Sarah, George F., James Frederick (who later stopped using his first name) and William Edwin. George worked in the mills for most of his life, and his two oldest surviving

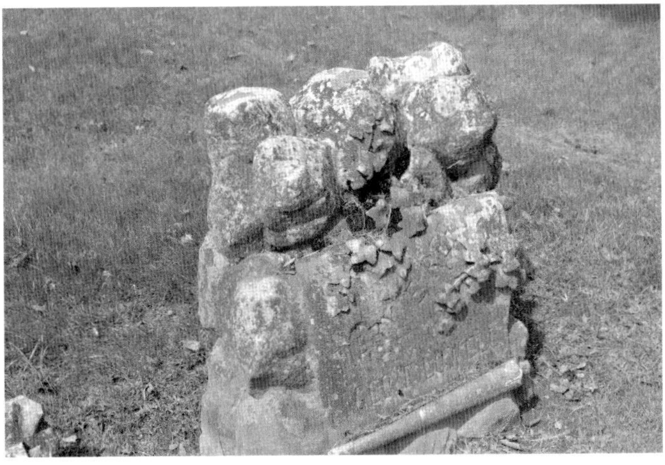

A marble stone carved to look like a naturalistic vine-draped stone wall. *Authors' collection.*

sons started there as well. Frederick relocated to Boston, where he worked as a clerk. He and Climenia were the parents of Bertha (who married Charles S. MacMillan and lived in Boston) and Reba Lowell. William also moved to Massachusetts.

After the death of his first wife, Ida, William married Elizabeth Hurley (who isn't buried in the plot). They were the parents of Lillian, Mabel, George W., William Jr. and Helen. William was a Boston policeman and died of a brain hemorrhage precipitated by acute bronchitis. Mary Ellen Reece was born in New Brunswick and married George F. Lowell in Saco. She was the mother of Charles P. Lowell (born in 1880), the infant George F. and a daughter, Ethel. Mary died in Boston of "phthisis," which was often another name for tuberculosis. That only leaves Frances M. Green, whose identity remains unknown. George and Mary Reece Lowell and their infant son have some of the more unusual gravestones that can be found in Laurel Hill Cemetery. Their names are casually scrawled across scrolls balanced on stones that are carved to look like naturalistic piles of stone!

JOHNSON, WALTER F. [FATHER], 22 APR 1836–27 JAN 1914
WILLIAM, D. 15 SEPT 1857, AGED 69 YRS.
BETSEY, WIFE OF WILLIAM JOHNSON, D. 22 OCT 1827, AGED 45 YRS.
ELLEN DICKINSON, DAU. OF JOHN AND BETSEY DICKINSON, D. 25 DEC 1818, AGED 3 YRS. 6 MOS.

William and Betsy Johnson share a gravestone—a very frugal way to mark their resting place. It's signed "Emery of Saco" and is one of the stones done by John F. Emery, who appeared on the 1860 Saco census as a thirty-nine-year-old "gravestone cutter." It seems as if the Johnson family never had much money. William was most likely the son of James Johnson of Biddeford. James's death is noted in the Saco book of vital records: "James a pauper of Biddeford died at his son William's 19 January 1817." William and his wife, Betsy, were parents to at least five little girls born in Saco: Rebecca (1809); Martha (1810); Betsy (1814), who later married John Dickinson; Charity (1819); and Sarah (1823.) They may also have been the parents of Lucy, whose death was noted in the record book in 1825 but whose birth wasn't recorded. William's wife, Betsy, died in 1827 (aged forty-three, not the forty-five that's reported in *York County Cemetery Inscriptions*), but William remarried a much younger woman (just twenty to twenty-nine in 1840) and had two more sons afterward: Charles, born in 1834, and Walter, born in 1836. Another note in the vital records book is of the death of Charity on January 23, 1834, "at the poorhouse." Charles drowned at the age of five. Unfortunately, William doesn't seem to have been counted in the 1850 census—the first census year that identifies family members by name—and that might have provided more information about his second wife and children.

When Walter died many years later, his death certificate said that his father had been a sailor—generally not a job that paid well. When Walter enlisted for a three-year term in the Civil War in October 1861, he was described as having fair skin and blue eyes and being five feet, eleven inches in height. He served his full enlistment in Company B of the First Maine Volunteer Infantry. In 1874, he was working in Boston as a brick mason when he married Margaret Gamble of New Brunswick. By the time of the 1900 census, Walter and his wife had returned to Maine and were living at $54\frac{1}{2}$ Portland Road in Saco with their youngest child, Arlington, who'd been born in 1887. In 1910, he was still living with them and working as a house carpenter. That census also reported that Walter and Margaret ("Nellie") had had four children, all living. Walter died of cirrhosis of the liver in 1914.

Saco's vital records identify an Ellen, the daughter of John and Betsy Dickinson, who was born on June 10, 1845. This is almost certainly the Ellen whose grave is with the Johnsons, with her death date misread in *York County Cemetery Inscriptions*. The only census that John and Betsy Dickinson could be found on was the 1870 census. The two families living with them were those of their married daughters, Eliza and Sarah. Eliza had done well by her marriage—her spouse, Frank Cleaves, had personal property worth $30,000 when he was just twenty-five. There's no record of him ever holding a job. Sarah had married a laborer, George Barrows. The other person in the household was Betsy's eldest sister, Rebecca, who was unmarried and working as a washerwoman—one of the very hardest (and often lowest-paying) jobs that was available to women of the era. Betsy had an unwed daughter, Lucy, at home, as well, working in the cotton mill. Betsy's husband, John Dickinson, had "no occupation," continuing the cycle of poverty that trapped most of the family.

SOUTH AND MAIN AVENUES

Moulton, Thomas T., d. 5 July 1834, aged 40 yrs.
Sarah P., wife of Thomas T. Moulton, d. 5 June 1874, aged 75 yrs.
Edward S., son of Thomas T. and Sarah P. Moulton, d. 3 Oct 1847, aged 22 yrs. 5 mos.
Benjamin P., d. 1 May 1864, aged 41
Sarah E., 10 Oct 1831–14 May 1885
Chisholm, Alexander F., d. 19 Nov 1871, aged 59 yrs. 1 mo.
Emilie F. Moulton, wife of Alexander F. Chisholm, d. 5 Aug 1913, aged 79 yrs. 3 mos.
Pike, Elizabeth H., dau. of Benjamin and Mary Pike, d. 2 Jan 1817, aged 12 yrs. 7 mos.
Hon. Benjamin, d. at Augusta, 14 Jan 1832, aged 62
Mary, wife of Hon. Benjamin Pike, d. 5 Apr 1820, aged 54

The Honorable Benjamin Pike began his career as a blacksmith in Saco with a shop at the corner of Main and School Streets. Later, he built a house attached to the shop that faced School Street. Long after Benjamin gave up being a blacksmith, the shop was still in operation. During one cold night in 1848, a blacksmith by the name of Dame, who worked there, froze to death in the shop. Benjamin served terms as town clerk, a town councilor and, finally, as a state senator. It was during his stint as senator that he died in Augusta in 1832. His gravestone was carved by Portland gravestone carver Francis Ilsley. Benjamin's daughter, Sarah

Philbrick Pike, married Thomas T. Moulton of Dover, who was the nephew of Edward S. Moulton, a prominent clockmaker who relocated to Saco in about 1813. The couple moved to Saco around the time of Benjamin Pike's death. Sarah had inherited a substantial portion of his many properties. Thomas joined Edward in his clock-making shop. While they meticulously crafted the brass clockworks, cabinetmaker Abraham Forsskol crafted the cases. Only one clock of Thomas's is known to still exist, although there may be many more; his uncle was far more prolific in the trade, however. Thomas died rather young—just six months after the birth of his youngest child, Emilie, who is buried here with her husband, Alexander Chisholm.

Also here are Benjamin's wife, Mary; another of their daughters, Elizabeth Howe Pike; Thomas's unmarried sister, Sarah; and two more of Thomas's children, Edward and Benjamin, who became a newspaper reporter and then an editor in Boston. Benjamin P. Moulton's large, ornate stone is signed on the left side of the bottom front. The faded name may be "Andrews, Leonard," who in 1860 was the twenty-four-year-old son of a Biddeford stonecutter, Ira Andrews, and who appeared on a list of stonecutters in the *1866 Saco City Directory*. Leonard didn't stay long in the business; for most of the rest of his life, he was a blacksmith.

Sweetser, Cornelius, b. Reading, Mass., 6 Apr 1808.

"He lived in Saco many years, dying there 20 Dec 1881. By his prudence, industry and wisdom he accumulated a large estate. He disposed of it for the education, support, happiness and good of many persons. His name is well worthy of lasting remembrance."

Maria, d. 1872

Born in Reading, Massachusetts, in 1846, Cornelius Sweetser moved to Saco with his wife, Nancy Wyman Richardson. On the 1860 census, he was listed as a shoe dealer with an estate valued at a very substantial $32,000. He also had three people boarding with him. In 1870, Cornelius was listed as a shoe manufacturer with an estate of $45,000, and living with him and his wife was Georgia Sweetser (a three-year-old child who doesn't seem to appear on any other records), as well as Maria Richardson, aged sixty-four, probably his sister-in-law (and the same Maria who was buried in his plot). By this time, he was active in politics, serving on the town council, as a county commissioner and in the Maine legislature.

His obituary noted, "He accumulated a large estate, and disposed of it for the education and good of many persons." During his lifetime, he was known for his philanthropic work, and many of the bequests he made continue to provide for Saco's citizens even 130 years after he died. He gave $10,000 to the York Institute and another $110,000 to other causes, including money to fund elaborate Pepperrell Park (largely obliterated when Fairfield School was constructed in about 1961). He lived in a large home with a mansard roof (which he added) on the east side of Main Street, near the corner with Beach Street. His wife, Nancy, lived on until 1898 and died of pneumonia in Ashland, Massachusetts.

FERNALD, NATHANIEL, D. 22 MARCH 1878, AGED 78 YRS. 8 MOS.
ELIZA H., D. 10 JAN 1886, AGED 79 YRS.
LABBY [*SIC*], MARY E. WIFE OF FRANK B. LABBY, D. 30 JAN 1871, AGED 32 YRS. 5 MOS.
LIBBY, EDGAR F., SON OF FRANK B. AND MARY E. LIBBY, D. 2 JUNE 1883, AGED 17 YRS. 10 MOS.
MARY E., DAU. OF FRANK B. AND MARY E. LIBBY, D. 3 JAN 1868, AGED 8 MOS.

Nathaniel Fernald Jr., the youngest of the four sons of Nathaniel and Sarah Fernald, was a sea captain. He and his wife seem to have been parents to just one daughter, Mary. According to John Haley, Nathaniel's wife, Eliza Tounge, frequently accompanied him when he sailed, but she stayed home for the last voyage the fair, five-foot-seven, blue-eyed Nathaniel would ever take. Encountering a violent storm, his ship was wrecked on rocks on the coast of Nova Scotia, with a total loss of ship and cargo. Nathaniel was washed ashore, but with both legs badly broken and the ship gone, he was reduced to poverty. Eliza took in washing to support them both. Unable to walk for many months, Nathaniel was able to help by sitting and pounding the clothes (the invention of real washing machines still being many years in the future). They were successful enough that they were able to build a small house on School Street that they enlarged in about 1850. Unable or unwilling to sail again, Nathaniel took up a second career of "wharfinger," operating a wharf. He also kept a sail loft (where sails were cut and stitched). No record could be found for the marriage of their daughter, Mary, to Frank B. Libby, but by 1870, Mary and her son, Edgar, were back living with her parents. After his mother died, Edgar lived with his grandmother for the rest of his brief life. By the time Eliza died in 1886, this hardworking woman had outlived all of her family.

MYERS, WILLIAM, ELDEST SON OF WILLIAM AND JANE MYERS, OF VICTORIA STREET, ASHTON-UNDER-LYNE, D. SACO, U.S.A., 17 SEPT 1871, AGED 24 YRS.

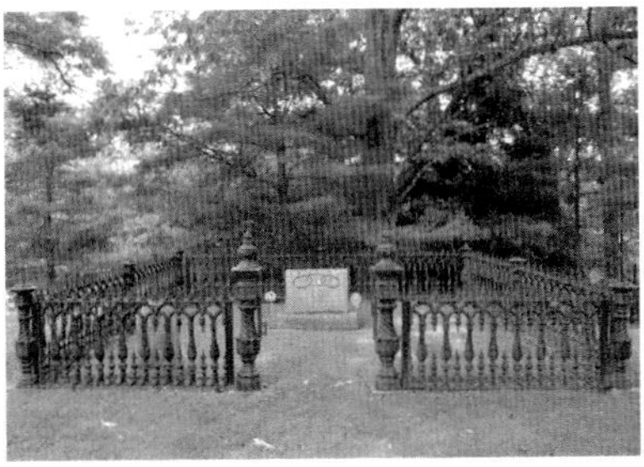

William Myers is buried in the beautifully fenced plot belonging to the Rebekahs, the female branch of the Independent Order of Odd Fellows. *Authors' collection.*

William, the eldest of the five children of William and Jane Whitehead Myers, came to the Saco/Biddeford area to work in the cotton mill. His father was also a cotton millworker back in England. Why William left distant England to do the very same work as his father is not known. Perhaps the elder Myers was a member of the Independent Order of Odd Fellows, which could help explain why William is buried here in this plot owned by the female branch of that fraternal order. Although his death was noted in the local newspaper, no cause was listed for this young man passing away so far from friends and family.

MORRILL, CAPT. SAMUEL J., D. 5 SEPT 1854, AGED 71
SARAH FROST, DAU. OF S.J. AND E.S. MORRILL, D. 10 OCT 1819, AGED 13 MOS.
GEORGE F., SON OF S.J. AND E.S. MORRILL, D. AT HAVANA, 5 NOV 1842
ABIGAIL, WIFE OF CAPT. SAMUEL J. MORRILL, D. 13 JAN 1813, AGED 29
ELIZA S., WIFE OF CAPT. SAMUEL J. MORRILL, D. 23 OCT 1832, AGED 35

Captain Samuel Jordan Morrill was born in April 1784, the son of Colonel Joseph Morrill and Mary Jordan. He married Abigail Dennett of Portsmouth, New Hampshire, in 1806. They had two children: Ann Maria, born in 1807, and Joseph, born in 1809. Abigail died in 1813. In 1816, the captain remarried, this time to Elizabeth S. Frost of Portsmouth. She was nineteen to his thirty-two. They had four children: Samuel, born in 1817; Sarah, born in 1818 (and buried here after she died at thirteen months); George, born in 1820, who died of yellow fever at the age of twenty-two in Havana; and Jonathan, born in 1822. A physician from Key West, T.A. Pinckney, wrote to the *American Journal of Medical Sciences* around the time of George's death to describe the management of yellow fever: "[T]he treatment recommended by our standard authorities—bleeding freely in the forming and first stages of the disease, active cathartics and the employment of such other remedies as the symptoms indicated," making it clear that a victim of the disease had little possibility of surviving "treatment." Yellow fever was endemic in Cuba throughout the nineteenth century and was one of many hazards sailors had to accept.

Both of the captain's wives are also buried here. According to Saco historian John Haley, Captain Morrill, near the end of his life, lived with his married daughter, Ann Hill, at the foot of Front Street. "If ever there was an old pirate, it was 'Old Jord. Morrill,' as he was called. He had a devil in him bigger than a mastodon, and he was a holy terror to the Saco urchin of those days. They used to go down there in squads to tantalize the old heathen, who 'raged' and imagined he was still on the high seas and could command, although he was powerless to do anything but 'fill the air' with imprecations."

Leland, Joseph W., d. 7 Sept 1858, aged 53
Hannah P., d. 17 Oct 1893, aged 77 [double stone with above]
Mr. Joseph, 30 Dec 1756–29 May 1839
"A soldier of the Revolution, active patriot, an honest man..."
Mrs. Dorcas, 20 May 1766–6 Oct 1833
Lucinda, dau. of Joseph and Dorcas Leland, d. 3 Oct 1816, aged 18
Joseph W., d. 21 March 1804
Dorcas K., d. 9 Sept 1862, aged 62 yrs.
Boynton, Benjamin Abbot, son of Abel and Sarah Boynton, d. 28 Jan 1815, aged 3 mos. 12 days

Joseph Leland was among the twelve children of Lydia Fletcher and Phineas Leland, a Grafton, Massachusetts farmer. Being a third son and unlikely to inherit the family farm, Joseph joined the Continental army at the outset of the Revolutionary War and rose from private to lieutenant. At the end of the war, he married Dorcas King and settled first in Scarborough and then in Phippsburg and finally relocated to Saco in about 1800, where he set about amassing wealth and a strong, positive reputation.

In about 1803, Joseph had a mansion designed for his family by Bradbury Johnson and built on Main Street. It was later the home of Sarah Fairfield Hamilton and still stands. On the last census before his death, Joseph W., Hannah and their daughter, Mary, were living in a large rooming house on Main Street, perhaps finding their mansion too hard to manage. According to *The Leland Magazine, or a Genealogical Record of Henry Leland and his Descendants*, "He was a judicious and discreet man; highly respected and much esteemed among the people of his acquaintance....He was a man of quiet, domestic habits, and sustained an irreproachable moral character."

John Haley, however, thought the man had a sense of humor. Haley said that "one of Saco's old jokers" played a trick on Joseph. He saw Leland sawing a wine pipe in half and then went down the street very seriously telling people that Mr. Leland had cut his wine pipe off, fully knowing that they were going to hear "wind pipe" and assume the man had cut his throat. Haley said that Leland greatly enjoyed the joke, since it was everyone else that'd been fooled, not him. He served two terms as a senator in the Massachusetts legislature (before Maine achieved statehood). Dorcas and Joseph had three sons (with just one living to adulthood) and seven daughters, with one, Lucinda, dying in her teens. Their remaining daughters married well and had successful progeny. Their eldest son, Cyrus King, died in 1790 before the family moved to Saco. Son Joseph Warren Leland attended Bowdoin College, studied to be a lawyer and married Hannah Scamman. They settled in Saco and had just one daughter. Tiny Benjamin Abbot Boynton was the son of Joseph and Dorcas's daughter Sarah and her husband, Abel Boynton, a lawyer from Bath, Maine.

Both Lucinda Leland's and Benjamin Boynton's stones were carved by Alvan Washburn, a Portland stone carver employed by Bartlett Adams (see *Early Gravestones in Southern Maine* by Ron Romano for much more about these two men). Joseph Jr.'s stone was also carved in that shop, but clues to the maker are more ambiguous.

NOYES, ISAAC BADGER, SON OF WILLIAM AND MARY J. NOYES, D. 30 DEC 1864, AGED 25 YRS. 4 MOS.

MARY ISABELLA, DAU. OF WILLIAM AND MARY JANE NOYES, D. 26 SEPT 1849, AGED 2 YRS. 7 MOS.

MARY MARIA, DAU. OF WILLIAM AND MARY JANE NOYES, D. 15 AUG 1846, AGED 5 YRS. 1 MO.

The gravestone of the Noyes daughters features a pair of clasped hands. The double stone marks the graves of Mary Maria, who was born in 1841 and died at the age of five, and her sister Mary Isabella, who was born the spring after her older sister's death. Did William and Mary Jane Noyes imagine

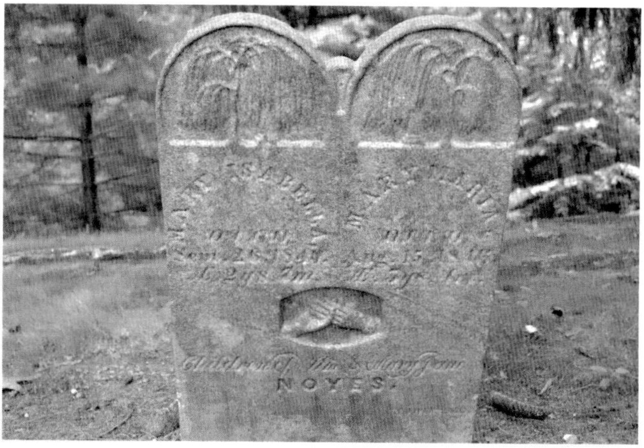

The willows on the headstone of the Noyes children have begun to melt away, but the clasped hands are still clearly visible. *Authors' collection.*

one Mary welcoming the other to heaven? Naming a child for one who was deceased seems rather morbid now, but at the time it was a very common way to honor a much-missed child. Isaac Badger Noyes was born in 1839 and may have been old enough to remember both of his sisters. In his short life, Isaac became a lawyer and served just two months at the opening of the Civil War in the summer of 1862 and then mustered out, perhaps due to ill health. He died just a few years later. The Noyes family would eventually have six children besides the two Marys: four boys and two more little girls. Buried only about two hundred feet away from this plot is their son William S. Noyes. A.E. Piper of Saco signed this stone.

GOOKIN, HANNAH E., DAU. OF WILLIAM AND CATHERINE GOOKIN, D. JAN 1843, AGED 9 MOS.

ELEANOR, DAU. OF WILLIAM AND CATHERINE GOOKIN, D. MARCH 1845, AGED 3 MOS.

LUCY E., DAU. OF DANIEL AND BETSEY GOOKIN, D. 6 SEPT 1849, AGED 14 YRS.

HANNAH, DAU. OF DANIEL AND BETSEY GOOKIN, AGED 4 YRS.

ISABEL, DAU. OF DANIEL AND BETSEY GOOKIN, AGED 2 YRS.

DANIEL, JR., D. 5 JULY 1854, AGED 18 YRS. 4 MOS.

LUCRETIA S., D. 9 DEC 1863, 35 YRS. 6 MOS. 25 DAYS

MARY S., D. 24 JULY 1864, AGED 41 YRS. 9 MOS. 3 DAYS

DANIEL, 1796–1873

BETSEY GOODWIN, WIFE OF DANIEL GOOKIN, 1799–1867

WILLIAM H., D. 10 JULY 1885, AGED 39 YRS.

"A MEM. OF CO. H, 2 REGT., ME CAV."

WILLIAM S., 1819–1900
CATHERINE BOWDOIN, WIFE OF WILLIAM S. GOOKIN, 1818–1906
AUGUSTUS W., 1850–1891
LUCRETIA E., 1858–1902

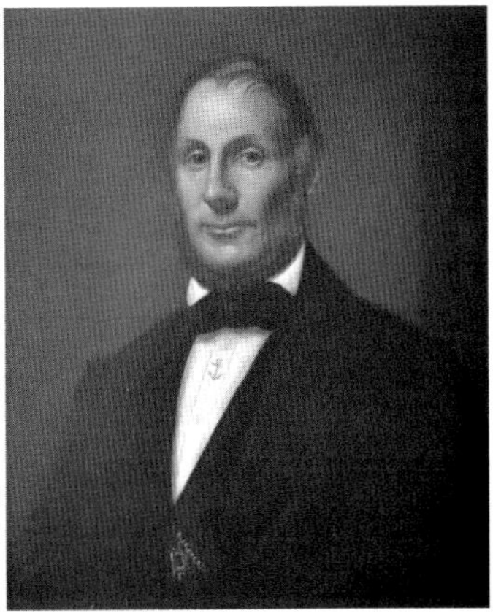
Daniel Gookin may (or may not) have ever been a ship's captain, but his shipbuilding skill certainly merited the anchor he proudly wore. *Collection of Saco Museum.*

Daniel Gookin lived most of his life in Biddeford, but he was born in New Hampshire. In his younger years, family legend says that he had been a ship's captain and that it was while working at this dangerous career that he lost a leg, wearing a wooden one for the rest of his life. That led to a career change as a shipbuilder. His younger brother was artist William Stoodley Gookin, but he was not the artist who completed Daniel's portrait. His family plot has a few especially interesting gravestones that are notable because of the very fancy font that was used on them. Although they're quite pretty, they convey tragedy. Daniel and Betsey were married in 1818. They seem to have had at least seven children, but they lived to see six of them *and* their granddaughter pass away. Their three youngest, Lucy, Hannah and Isabel, all died very young; their son Daniel as a teenager; and their two oldest daughters, Lucretia S. and Mary S., in young adulthood, one of heart disease and the other of "debility." Their son William S. was a sea captain. He and his wife, Catherine, had eight children. Three of their children—Hannah, Eleanor and George—all died as very young children. Lucretia, Augustus and William H. died in early adulthood. Only Adelbert and Mary survived their parents. William S. Gookin died of "congestion of the lungs" but had only been sick eighteen hours when he passed away.

CRAIG, SAMUEL H., 31 OCT 1861–1 JUNE 1929. V.F.W.
CAROLINE DEVEREUX, WIFE OF SAMUEL H, CRAIG, DAU. OF JOHN AND REBECCA MELLEN, RICHMOND, VA., 11 FEB 1861–DURHAM, N.H., 14 AUG 1931
MELLEN, REBECCA CALVERT, NORFOLK, VA., 11 DEC 1834–DURHAM, N.H., 23 JULY 1919

CAPT. HENRY B. U.S.A., 2 MARCH 1828–20 JUNE 1906
JOHN PRENTISS, 2ND SON OF JOHN AND REBECCA C. MELLEN, RICHMOND, VA., 14 FEB 1863–26 NOV 1864; BUR. IN HOLLYWOOD CEMETERY, RICHMOND, VA.
JOHN P., DOVER, N.H., 21 MARCH 1799–DURHAM, N.H. 16 APR 1877
MEHITABLE SHEAFE, WIDOW OF JOHN P. MELLEN, NORTHWOOD, N.H., 20 AUG 1799–DURHAM, N.H., 27 MARCH 1879
MARGARET ANN, 20 APR 1824–20 JULY 1825
ELIZABETH ROLLINS, 4 APR 1833[?]–11 OCT 1847
FRANK PLUMER, SON OF JOHN P. AND M.S. MELLEN, 15 DEC 1837–13 OCT 1853, AGED 15 YRS. 10 MOS.
CAROLINE H., D. AT DOVER, N.H., 15 OCT 1859
JOHN, SACO, 29 SEPT 1829–CONCORD, N.H., 6 JUNE 1870
FRANK, SON OF JOHN AND R.C. MELLEN, D. 25 JULY 1859, AGED 1 MO.

Laurel Hill Cemetery is the final resting place of Medal of Honor winner Samuel H. Craig. He was born in New Market, New Hampshire, in 1863. On May 15, 1886, he was serving as a sergeant in the Fourth U.S. Cavalry in what would become Arizona. A band of Apaches had stolen a few dozen horses from a local rancher. Craig's company tracked the Native Americans into the nearby mountains and eventually found their encampment, attacked and took back the stolen animals, as well as quite a few horses and mules that belonged to the Apaches. In order to make their way back to their fort, they would have to travel for more than a day in heat through a parched landscape. Their lieutenant led them to a spring he knew of at the bottom of a steeply sided canyon. Unfortunately, the Apaches not only knew of the spring but also knew how to get there faster and were waiting on the high ground as the soldiers watered the animals. During the attack that followed, the horses bolted. Craig, although severely wounded, was able to stop their stampede, the act for which he received the Medal of Honor.

Up until World War I, the Medal of Honor was the only medal that was given to recognize bravery or meritorious service. When regulations were changed in the early twentieth century, some Medals of Honor were actually recalled, including those given to nearly the entire Twenty-Seventh Maine, members of which agreed to stay on a few days past their muster-out date to defend Washington, D.C., during the Battle of Gettysburg—not heroic, just inconvenient.

After his service, Craig returned to New Hampshire, where he seems to have lived for the rest of his life. Buried next to Samuel and his wife, Caroline, are the Mellen family, who are Caroline's parents and other relatives. Her grandparents, John and Mehitable, were both born in New Hampshire, but all of their six sons and one daughter were born in Saco. Caroline's father left Saco in young adulthood, so this was never her home.

HANSON, EDWIN W., 1 SEPT 1820–2 MARCH 1895
ALMIRA, WIFE OF EDWIN W. HANSON, 1822–1848
DRUSELLAR A., WIFE OF EDWIN W. HANSON, 1829–1878
ALBERT B., SON OF EDWIN W. HANSON, 1860–1885, BURIED AT KITTERY, ME.
ANNIE L., DAU. OF EDWIN W. HANSON, 1862–1872
HENRY C., SON OF EDWIN W. HANSON, 1856–1857
SUSIE J., WIFE OF EDWIN W. HANSON JR., 19 DEC 1851–28 JUNE 1894
CARRIE E., WIFE OF EDWIN W. HANSON JR., 1866–1928
WALTER E., SON OF EDWIN W. AND SUSIE J. HANSON, 1873–3 SEPT 1875, AGED 1 YR. 7 MOS.
HAROLD H., SON OF EDWIN W. AND SUSIE J. HANSON, 1879–1931

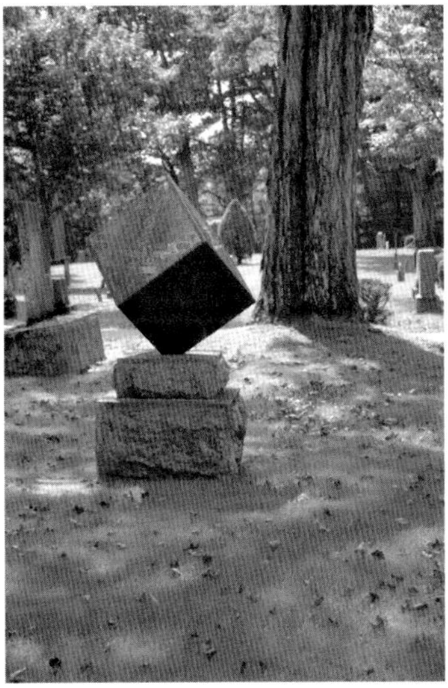

The Hanson gravestone appears to defy gravity. *Authors' collection.*

The Hanson family may have the most unusual and eye-catching memorial in the entire cemetery. This polished granite cube, balanced on a point, seems to defy gravity. Edwin Winslow Hanson was born in Windham, the son of Thomas and Hannah Gowen Hanson. He first married Almira Knight, the mother of Edwin Jr., who was born in about 1846. After Almira passed away, only twenty-six, Edwin married Drucilla Roberts in Westbrook, probably sometime shortly after the 1850 census was taken. In 1850, he and his young son, Edwin Jr., were living with Levi Hanson, Edwin's brother, in Biddeford, and Edwin was working as a laborer. Later, he would become a stonemason and move to Saco, where he lived for about a decade before moving to Elm Street in Biddeford after Drucilla died. Albert, Edwin and Drucilla's son, died only a year after marrying Lucy Kimball.

Edwin's only other surviving son, Edwin Jr., initially married Susan, the mother of Harold and Walter, born in Brunswick, where Edwin Jr. worked in the mill. By the time Susan died, Edwin Jr. had become a machinist and moved to Westbrook. Edwin Sr. was staying at his house when he died of heart disease in 1895. In 1899, Edwin Jr. married Carrie Emma Couch. They had no children. As late as 1920, Edwin was still working in a mill and living on Rochester Street in Westbrook. Perhaps it was he who ordered the elaborate monument (it appears too modern to have been crafted at the time of his father's death). Harold was the last to be buried in the plot. He, too, became a machinist and moved to New Jersey, where he fathered a child, also named Edwin Winslow Hanson.

MELLEN, CAROLINE MATILDA, WIFE OF GEORGE F. MELLEN, DAU. OF JOHNSON AND MARGARET LUNT, B. ME, 13 MARCH 1827, D. MISSISSIPPI, 2 AUG 1853 [ERECTED BY HER FATHER, JOHNSON LUNT, IN 1854]
"HER REMAINS TAKEN HOME BY HER EVER DEVOTED FATHER."
LUNT, HARRIET M. FORRSKOL, WIFE OF JOHNSON LUNT, 31 JULY 1832–29 FEB 1892

George F. Mellen was the eldest son of John P. and Mehitable Sheafe Mellen, who are buried not far from where Caroline lies. George was born and grew up in Saco. He graduated from Bowdoin College in 1846, taught school in Saco for a time, became a physician (a much shorter process in about 1850 than it is now) and relocated to Yazoo City, Mississippi, where he remained for the rest of his life. Caroline Matilda was the daughter of Saco merchant Johnson Lunt and his first wife, Margaret. She and George were married on April 6, 1852, and Caroline then accompanied her husband back to Yazoo City, located on the Mississippi River in west-central Mississippi.

In 1853, New Orleans was hit with a yellow fever epidemic that then traveled up the river, reaching Yazoo City. At the time, no one knew how yellow fever was spread, but people thought it was contagious and was caught from those who were sick with it. (In fact, it's spread by mosquitoes that have bitten victims and then bite others.) George would have been constantly busy treating victims, most of whom would die anyway (treatments of the time were very ineffective). With her death coming in the midst of the epidemic, it's very likely that Caroline succumbed to yellow fever. George would have believed that he brought the disease home to her. He never remarried and spent the rest of his life in Mississippi, dying in 1877. "Her remains taken home by her ever devoted father" seems to convey a sense of her father's love and loss but also anger at how she had died so far from home—and not been returned there by her husband.

Johnson Lunt was born in Clinton, Maine, and first married Margaret Foster Reed of Topsham. Through about 1830, he remained in Clinton and may have been the father of at least one son and five daughters, two of whom were Caroline and Elizabeth. Later, Johnson becomes harder to track down, until he suddenly reappears, noted in an 1849 city directory as living in Biddeford and selling lumber. He was counted on the 1860 census, living alone in Saco and selling crockery. After Margaret died, Johnson married Harriet M. Forrskol, the daughter of Swedish cabinetmaker Abraham Forrskol. On the 1870 census, it was Harriet who owned their home and the largest part of their personal property—a very unusual situation for the time. She must have brought her own property to the marriage. When she was counted on the 1880 census, living alone on Cross Street, she told the census taker that she was a widow, but she was no longer using the Lunt surname; she had become a Forrskol again. She was already listed as an invalid due to heart disease, but she lived on for another twelve years afterward.

Biglow, Lucy, relict of Amos Biglow, Esq., late of Weston, Mass., d. 6 Jan 1834, aged 72

Thacher, James Francis, son of George and Lucy B. Thacher, d. 28 Dec 1831, aged 3 yrs. 3 mos.

Emery, Elizabeth Marble, wife of George F. Emery, d. 28 Aug 1847, aged 24 yrs. 11 mos.

Emery, Lucy Bigelow, only dau. of George F. and E.M.C. Emery, d. Sept. 1849, aged 7 yrs.

Lucy Bigelow, only dau. of I. and F.S. Emery, 1824–1834

Faith S., wife of Isaac Emery, 1793–1834

Sarah Spring, wife of Isaac Emery, 1797–1876

Lucy Biglow, whose name was used several times in the next few generations—surely to honor a beloved lady—is buried under an attractive slate stone that has the traditional curved top with shoulders that was no longer especially stylish by the time of her death in 1834. However, the weeping willow carved on it was a more modern reminder of the sadness of death (that had by then fully replaced the more threatening death's head as a popular motif). Her stone was carved by Francis Ilsley, who was the last apprentice of carver Bartlett Adams in Portland, Maine. Lucy was originally interred in the Pepperrell burying ground. Born Lucy Savage, she married Amos Biglow in Weston, Massachusetts, where he was a successful merchant. They had had one son, Amos, and four daughters, Anna, Sarah, Lucy 2nd and Faith, by the time of his early death in 1794 at the age of thirty-four. ("Relict" is an early word for widow.)

Lucy 2nd, daughter of Lucy and Amos, married her first cousin, George Thacher, and her young son, James Francis, is buried here. She had five other children by the time of her death in Belfast in 1843.

Lucy and Amos's daughter Faith married Isaac Emery in Saco in 1819. Emery was a well-off merchant, served in the state legislature and was one of the first directors of Saco and Biddeford Savings Institution. Faith was the mother of George Frederick, William H. and little Lucy 3rd Bigelow. Lucy; her daughter Faith; and Faith's daughter, Lucy 3rd, all died in 1834. By 1850, Isaac had relocated to Boston, where he became even wealthier, dying there on July 3, 1875.

Faith's son George Emery married first Elizabeth Marble, the daughter of Antipas Marble and Sally Putnam of Cornish, New Hampshire, who was the younger sister of a classmate of George's at Thornton Academy and who later attended the school herself. She died in Boston of consumption in 1847 but is buried here. He married a second time, but that spouse's identity is unknown. Finally, when he was forty-eight, he married one more time, to a twenty-two-year-old. George seems to have lived most of his adult life in Massachusetts. He might be the man of that name who was living in a large boardinghouse in Pepperell, Massachusetts, in 1855 and who listed his job as "gentleman." He died in Boston of apoplexy in 1885.

Watson, James, d. 7 Sept 1849, aged 41 yrs.

Mary J., dau. of James and Belinda Watson, 30 May 1838–4 Dec 1854

Belinda M., dau. of James and Belinda Watson, 25 May 1841–18 Sept 1844

Staples, Belinda, widow of James Watson, wife of Mark Staples, d. 19 Sept 1878, aged 65 yrs.

Barker, James L., d. 20 July 1869, aged 42 yrs.

Martha G. Watson, wife of James L. Barker, 18 Apr 1835–18 Jan 1928

Goodwin, Barbara, dau. of Samuel and Martha Goodwin, Limington, 5 Nov 1807–Biddeford, 29 Apr 1866

The Watson family plot is surrounded by an impressive naturalistic wrought-iron fence that must have been a thing of beauty before it was so eroded by time. Composed of posts that are made to look like tree trunks and rails that resemble leafy branches, it seems to have had an arbor-like arch over the gateway. Fences like this were once very common in the cemetery; this is one of the few remaining. Those buried within have a complex series of relationships. James Watson was a machinist who lived on Summer Street in Saco before his early death. The year after he died, his widow, Belinda, was operating a boardinghouse for female mill operatives in Biddeford. On the 1860 census, she had remarried to Biddeford boot maker Mark Staples, who was himself the widower of Belinda's sister, Ann (called "Sally"). Belinda was laid to rest with her first husband. Mark, who died in 1880, was buried at Woodlawn Cemetery with Sally and their son.

Martha G. Watson was one of James and Belinda's children. Her husband, James Lewis Barker—a cabinetmaker and then a maker of pianofortes in Boston—first married Miriam Goodwin, who was the daughter of Belinda's father's half-brother. Miriam gave birth to one son and then died before 1859, when James married Martha. They had no surviving children. After James died, Martha moved back in with her mother. Once her mother had

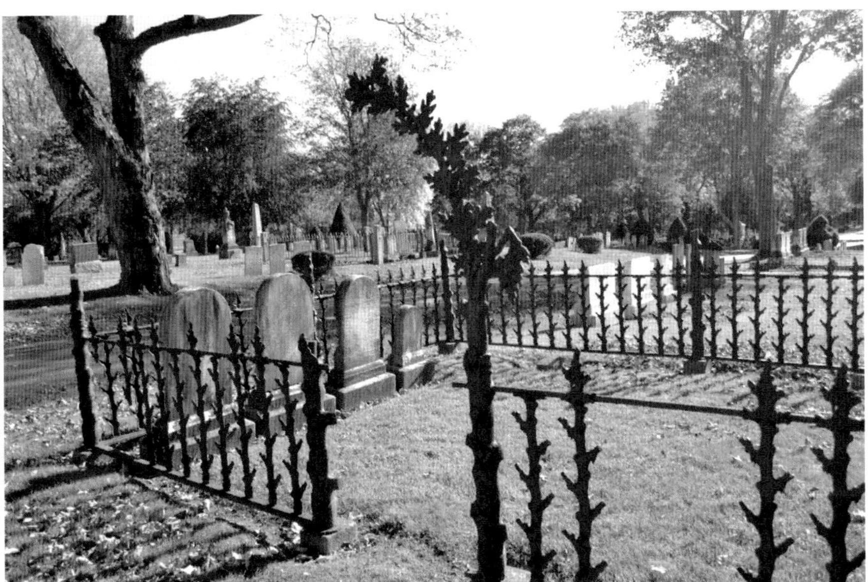

The fence around the Watson plot is badly damaged, but it's still a vivid reminder of its former splendor. *Authors' collection.*

passed away, Martha lived alone for the rest of her very long life. Barbara Goodwin was another of Belinda's sisters and never married. Although they purchased a cemetery plot and surrounded it with an expensive fence, none of the family was ever well-to-do.

SHANNON, RICHARD CUTTS, M.D., 10 AUG 1773–26 APR 1828, AGED 54 YRS. 8 MOS. 16 DAYS

MARY, WIFE OF RICHARD CUTTS SHANNON, M.D., D. 11 AUG 1821, AGED 45 YRS.

TEBBETS, CAROLINE, FORMERLY OF DOVER, N.H., D. 29 AUG 1813, AGED 19 YRS.

ABIGAIL, FORMERLY OF DOVER, NH, D. 29 AUG 1803, AGED 17 YRS.

Richard Cutts Shannon was born in Stratham County, New Hampshire, on August 10, 1773. He was the son of Thomas and Lillas Shannon. According to a local history, he graduated from Harvard College in 1795 and then spent a period of time studying medicine. He served in the U.S. Navy for a few years before coming to Saco in 1800. On July 11, 1801, he married Mary Tebbetts of Dover. Caroline and Abigail were Mary's younger sisters and died of consumption, according to letters later written by Mary's daughter. Three of Richard's nine children—Caroline, who died in 1803; Richard, who died in 1809; and Samuel Tibbets, who died in 1812—are also buried here. Richard and Mary would name later children for all three of those who died so young. Mary died in August 1821 of "quick consumption," and in December, Richard remarried to another Mary, the widow of Dr. Thomas Buckminster, the other physician in Saco at that time.

By many accounts, this was an unhappy marriage. While Mary Tebbets Shannon was considered a mild, gentle and even-tempered person, Mary Buckminster was not. Their son, the Richard C. Shannon who is buried next to the Deerings' grave plot, was born just five years before Richard Sr. died very suddenly of a stroke ("a shock of the numb palsy") at the age of fifty-five, leaving his second wife as the "uncomfortable stepmother of six children." Although the Shannon plot also includes a rather badly eroded marble obelisk, Shannon's own gravestone is a marvel of stone carving, with remarkably fine and very artful detail, done by an unidentified carver. His epitaph, composed by Cynthia Locke, the sister of Shannon's daughter Abigail's future husband, sums up his value to those who knew him:

While memory brings each kindly virtue near
That warmed the Heart now cold and lifeless here
And friendship mourns with dim and tearful eye
That one so loved in life so soon should die
Faith sends on high a wondering grateful song
That one so fit for Heaven was spared so long.

All of these people were originally interred in the Pepperrell burying ground and moved to Laurel Hill Cemetery.

PAUL, OTIS S., D. 20 FEB. 1852, AGED 24 YRS.
ELEANOR J., DAU. OF OTIS S. AND ROSANNA PAUL, D. 25 AUG. 1851, AGED 3 MOS. 11 DAYS
JOSHUA, D. 30 AUG 1857, AGED 60 YRS.
LORING M., SON OF JOSHUA AND JANE R. PAUL, D. 19 MARCH 1852, AGED 20 YRS. 8 MOS.
WILLIAM F., SON OF JOSHUA AND JANE R. PAUL, D. 10 OCT. 1833, AGED 3 YRS.
SILAS M., D. 1 FEB 1862, AGED 19 YRS. 2 MOS.
CARRIE M., D. 29 MARCH 1858, AGED 21 YRS. 5 MOS.
RACHEL S., D. 31 OCT 1864, AGED 20 YRS. 2 MOS.

The Paul family plot is across the avenue from the Shannon plot, in the second row. Joshua Paul was a "dyer" in the cotton mill. When the 1850 census captured a snapshot of his large family, they were living at 33 Temple Street in Saco. He and his wife, Jane Robinson Macomber, had nine children at home. Otis had already married; he was working in the mill but still living with his parents, perhaps because his health had

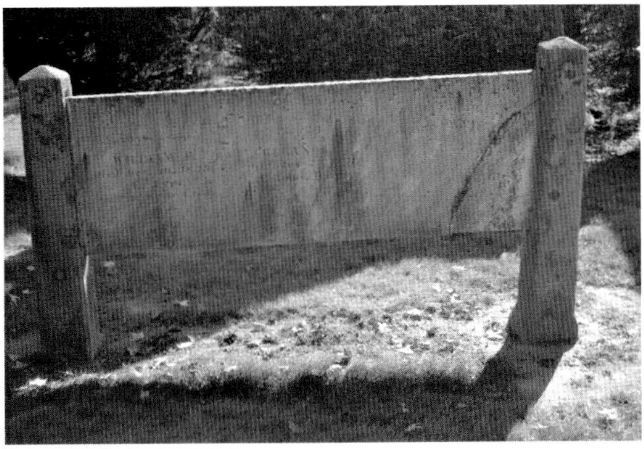

The Pauls' "billboard" gravestone is rare; just a few of these were ever erected. *Authors' collection.*

already begun to fail. He died of consumption just a month before his next younger brother, Loring, was lost to the same disease. In 1857, it would claim Joshua as well. In November 1861, Silas enlisted as a private in Company B of the U.S. Engineers and was sent to Washington, D.C., where he would only serve for a few months before dying of "typhoid pneumonia." Carrie's cause of death was also recorded as consumption, and it's very likely that it killed Rachel, too.

All of their tragic deaths are recorded on a very unusual "billboard monument"—one of only two in Laurel Hill. Not only were these never especially popular choices for markers, but they have also turned out to be particularly fragile. Cracks in the marble can cause the whole monument to break and collapse. The other such stone is located in the far back southeast corner of the cemetery, alongside a ravine.

TOPPAN, GEORGE H., SON OF GEORGE TOPPAN, D. 27 DEC 1827, AGED 4 YRS. 5 MOS.

ELIZABETH H., WIFE OF GEORGE TOPPAN, D. 14 JULY 1827, AGED 32 YRS.

ABIGAIL H., DAU. OF GEORGE TOPPAN, D. 5 NOV 1826, AGED 15 MOS.

FANNY, DAU OF GEORGE AND SHUAH TOPPAN, D. 23 JAN 1843, AGED 14 YRS. 9 MOS. 3 DAYS

WILLIAM, SON OF GEORGE AND SHUAH TOPPAN, D. 18 DEC 1842, AGED 9 YRS. 1MO.

JOSEPH, SON OF GEORGE AND SHUAH TOPPAN, D. 16 MARCH 1841, AGED 1 YR. 10 MOS.

JOHN, SON OF GEORGE AND SHUAH TOPPAN, D. 19 MAY 1839, AGED 3 DAYS

An unusual monolith marks the graves of the Tappan (or Toppan) family, just behind the Paul family plot. George H. Tappan, a farmer, was born in Newbury, Massachusetts, on November 9, 1794. He and his first wife, Elizabeth, were parents to at least two children: George, who was born in 1823, and Abigail, born in 1825. Her death is noted in the vital records of Saco ("child of George Tappan died"). Little George died the following winter, only a few months after the death of his mother. Just two weeks before his son's death, George had remarried to Shuah Libby, the daughter of Joseph and Shuah Libby, who are buried next to the Toppans. George and Shuah had a daughter, Fanny, in 1828, and sons George (in 1830), Daniel (in 1832), William (in 1833), Charles (in 1836) and twins Joseph and John (in May 1839). Little John lived just a few days; Joseph only lived to the age of two. Fanny died at the age of fourteen and William at the age of nine—all of their deaths in just about three years. So, of his nine children, George saw just three live to adulthood. Of those, only Daniel remained in Saco. He appeared on the 1870 census working as a farmer, married and the father of two school-aged children. Shuah and George senior are not buried in Laurel Hill—or at least not in marked graves.

Granger, Angelica K., d. 31 Dec 1917, aged 64 yrs., 2 mos.
Mary A. [Mother], d. 2 Apr 1889, aged 77 yrs., 3 mos.
Charles H. [Father], d. 5 Sept 1893, aged 80 yrs., 8 mos.

To the right of the Toppan family plot is that of the Granger clan. Charles Henry Granger was a local artist. Early in his career, he advertised that he no longer wished to paint postmortem portraits of the newly deceased. He'd only be willing to do these if he could work from a photograph. The Saco Museum has several attractive works by Granger in its collection, but he never achieved national recognition. The Grangers had two daughters and a son. Their son died in the Civil War, and one daughter died just five years later. On the 1880 census, Angelica had returned home to 9 Summer Street in Saco, where in city directories she was listed as an artist.

John Haley wasn't fond of the Grangers, noting, "Mr. Granger was not especially fortunate in his descendants, their mental equipment was in some degree juggled. One became violently insane, the other less so. The latter [Charles Henry Granger] was a whilom musician, poet, and artist, who found it very difficult to assimilate with the common herd. His daughter is a victim of the disease known as 'garrulous,' and is much gifted with small talk. She admits 'the weather is bad,' but hastens to divest herself of any responsibility in the matter. She also indulged the amiable fiction that she is an artist, of much merit. Conditions are such that her tribe will not increase." For many years, Charles kept a diary in which he was often rather disdainful of many he encountered, a judgment that perhaps Haley (and others) noticed.

EAST AVENUE

Calef, Josiah, d. 2 March, 1863, aged 80 yrs. 9 mos. 11 days
Susan H., wife of Josiah Calef, d. 10 March 1822, aged 32 yrs.
Sarah P., wife of Josiah Calef, d. 24 Apr 1878, aged 85 yrs. 3 mos. 20 days
Mary, d. 10 Feb 1845, aged 25 yrs.
George F., son of Josiah and Sarah P. Calef, 1829–1891
Frances Thornton, wife of George F. Calef, 1 Aug 1837–16 May 1904
R.G. [footstone only]
George Thornton, son of G.F. and F. Calef, 1871
Mabel, dau. of G.F. and F. Calef, 1878
Bartlett, Albert, d. 8 March 1842, aged 26 yrs. 6 mos.
Cutts, S.A. Bartlett, dau. of Josiah and Susan Calef, d. 23 Nov 1889

Josiah Calef, the first chairman of the trustees of Laurel Hill Cemetery, was a wealthy man but not always a very happy person. The son of Joseph Calef and Miriam Bartlett of Kingston, New Hampshire, Josiah had come to Saco by about 1800. He first married Susan Hussey of Nantucket. Together they had five daughters and three sons before Susan died about two weeks after the birth of their youngest child, Josiah. Five years later, he remarried to a woman from Kingston, Sarah Phillips Gale. She would have two more children, a son and a daughter. Around 1811, Josiah collaborated with merchant and all-round entrepreneur Thomas Cutts to build a nail factory on Factory Island. Like almost everything Cutts touched, it was highly successful.

Later, Josiah would operate a hardware store. It's impossible to know what led to Josiah's depression, but sometime in middle age, he attempted suicide. He used a knife to cut his throat, and then, perhaps concerned that he hadn't fully accomplished the deed, plunged his head into a tub of water, planning to drown himself if he didn't bleed to death first. In the end, neither one happened. He passed out and then fell out of the tub. The cold water apparently helped stop his bleeding, and he made a full recovery—except for having a very prominent scar on his neck. According to John Haley, he wore a high collar and stock for the rest of his life to hide the scar—although Saco being a small town, everyone knew it was there.

Josiah's daughter Susan first married Albert Gallatin Bartlett, who was her grandmother's nephew. He lived only a few years, and then she married Thomas Cutts Jr., the son of her father's partner. Josiah's son George took over business when his father passed away, but farming was more to his liking. He and Frances Thornton, the daughter of James Brown Thornton and Elizabeth Gookin, had three children before George died relatively young; the only one of their children who survived was Ralph Gookin Calef, who relocated to the Boston area. He is most likely the "R.G." who has a footstone but no headstone.

NYE, SAMUEL, 1778–1826
EUNICE C., WIFE OF SAMUEL NYE
CAROLINE A. DAU. OF SAMUEL NYE AND EUNICE C. NYE, 1811–1816
BENJAMIN B., SON OF SAMUEL NYE AND EUNICE C. NYE, 1822–1822
CHARLOTTE, DAU. OF SAMUEL NYE AND EUNICE C. NYE, 1823–1823
SAMUEL, SON OF SAMUEL NYE AND EUNICE C. NYE, 1814–1844
JOSEPH T., SON OF SAMUEL NYE AND EUNICE C. NYE, 1819–1859
CHARLES A., SON OF SAMUEL NYE AND EUNICE C. NYE, 1816–1866
DOMINICUS C., SON OF SAMUEL NYE AND EUNICE C. NYE, 1824–1889
EUNICE C., DAU. OF SAMUEL NYE AND EUNICE C. NYE, 1807–1889
MARY E., DAU. OF SAMUEL NYE AND EUNICE C. NYE, 1806–1890
ANN M., DAU. OF SAMUEL NYE AND EUNICE C. NYE, 1808–1891

Eunice Cutts was born in Saco but sent by her parents to a female boarding school in the Boston area, probably where she met Samuel Nye. The son of Joseph Nye and Mary Winslow, Samuel was born in Harwich, Massachusetts. They were married in 1803. Eunice's wealthy parents, Thomas and Elizabeth Cutts, were eager to have the couple return home—perhaps aware that they were already struggling financially—and offered to build a house for them. The Nyes moved to Saco in 1812, and the large home was constructed at the corner of North and Elm Streets in Saco but later moved to 17 Clark Street (where it still stands). According to John Haley, Eunice Cutts Nye was required to return to her father the silver that she'd been given at the time of her marriage in exchange for his construction of their home. Haley claims that when Thomas died, Eunice immediately took back the silver. This would've taken place a few decades before Haley was born, so it may reflect more the stories that were told about the Nyes than the truth. Several years before his death, Eunice's father composed a document (in the collection of the Saco Museum) that meticulously recorded the exact amount of money each of his children had already received, so that their varied inheritances from him, he said, would be equitable to all.

Samuel served for a time as a major in the army during the War of 1812 but died in 1826, leaving Eunice to find a way to support her large brood. Haley also wrote that some years after Samuel died, when his youngest daughter, Ann, was fully grown, tax collector David Tuxbury visited the Nye home seeking their tax payment. Ann remarked that she had "a vision from God, who told her not to pay the taxes." Tuxbury replied, "I had a vision or word from the same authority, telling me to put you in jail." Ann supposedly then promptly paid her taxes. Of the ten Nye children, only Mary and Dominicus married—Mary to James Snow, who died in Florida at a rather young age, leaving her with just one daughter, Cecillia. On the 1850 census, the two of them were boarding with the Hights. Daughter Eunice 2nd was briefly courted by her first cousin, William Cutts (who was himself the son of first cousins) after his first wife (*also* a first cousin), Elizabeth Cutts Thornton, died. Eunice rejected his attentions. Haley claimed that she said, "There are enough fools in the family now." Samuel's wife, Eunice, died in 1853. As the Nye offspring grew older, they retired to the Clark Street home and lived out their lives in increasing poverty, keeping the doors and windows closed up, rarely going visiting and refusing what few callers they had—apparently too proud and independent to reveal their destitution.

Cutts, Col. Thomas, d. 10 Jan. 1821, aged 85 yrs.
Elizabeth, wife of Col. Thomas Cutts, d. 11 Jan 1803, aged 57 yrs.

Thomas and Elizabeth Cutts are also buried here, although they were first interred in their family mausoleum in the Pepperrell burying ground. They're

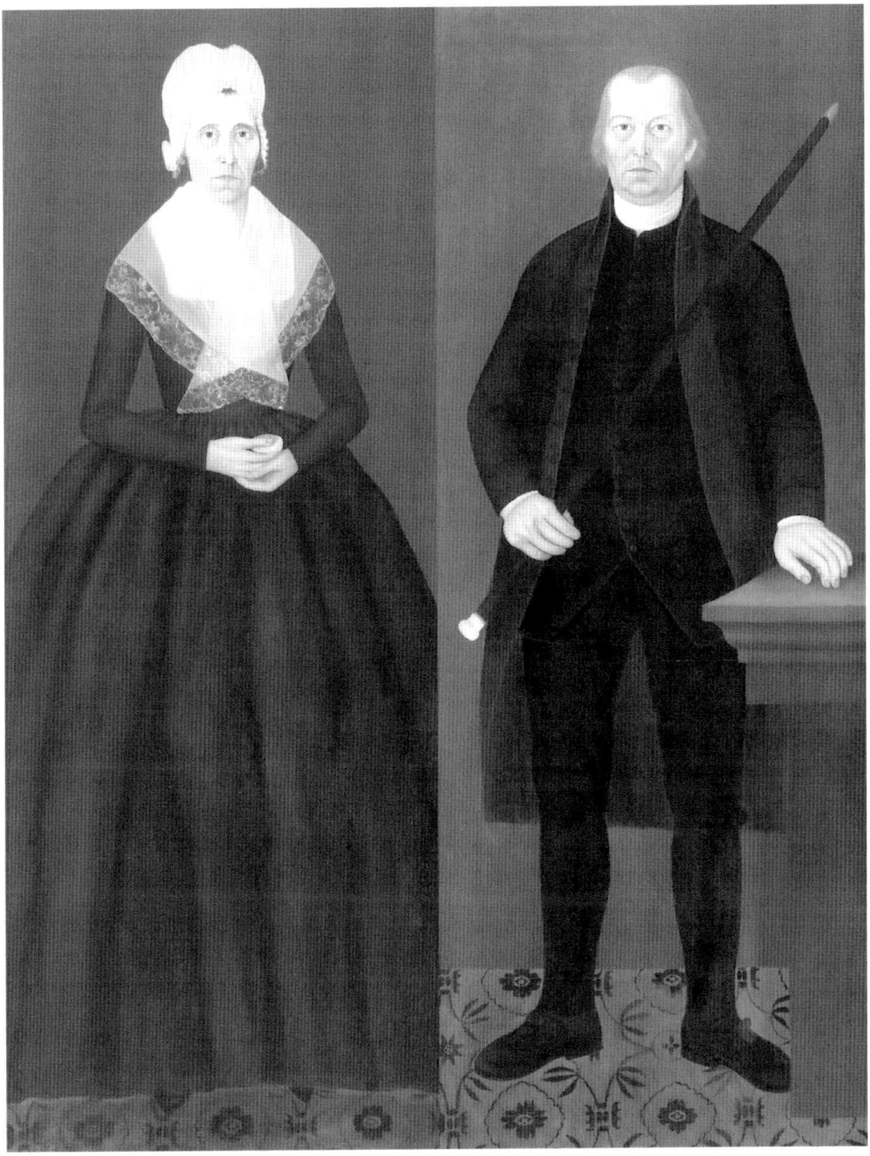

Well-dressed Thomas and Elizabeth Cutts leave no doubt of their significant role in the community. *Collection of Saco Museum.*

the subjects of the full-length portraits by deaf-mute artist John Brewster Jr. that hang in the front gallery of the Saco Museum. Thomas was born in 1736 into a very wealthy Kittery family. Descriptions of his youth include a "lordly" domain on an island in the Piscataqua River, Sunday soirees by invitation only, a staff of dairy maids and even a pleasure boat. Thomas, however, was the ninth of ten children, so he couldn't expect to inherit this degree of wealth.

At the age of twenty-two, backed with a hefty $100 on loan from his father, he settled in Saco. Records note that he "had a good head for business" and quickly repaid his debt. Recognizing the important location of what would become Cutts Island, in the middle of the Saco River between two growing towns, he began to buy up that land. He built a small house and store on the southwest end of the island. A new bridge greatly enhanced his business prospects. In 1775, he purchased a much larger part of the island from the estate of his mentor, Sir William Pepperrell. In 1762, Thomas married Elizabeth Scammon. He was twenty-six to her seventeen. They took up residence in that small house and lived there for the next twenty years while their family expanded to include eight children and their wealth multiplied exponentially.

Finally, in 1782, he erected a large, gambrel-roofed three-story mansion on the hill on Cutts Island that in the early nineteenth century was the most highly taxed home in York County. (In the twentieth century, it was taken apart and reassembled, less one story, on Glenhaven Circle.) With business thriving, he bought vast tracts of land. He was a founder of the Saco Bank and formed the Saco Iron Works Company, which made huge quantities of nails. He was a selectman, town treasurer, representative to the General Court, councilor of Massachusetts and a Revolutionary War officer. He donated a Paul Revere bell to the First Parish Meeting House when it was constructed in 1806. He seems to have been well loved by his children. When Thomas died in 1821, he left a sizable estate.

The portrait John Brewster Jr. painted of him was done in 1795, when Cutts was at the height of his career. It's one of only two known full-sized, full-length portraits that Brewster painted. Cutts stands next to a table, one hand casually atop it, the other clutching a cane. He's dressed in dark, somber clothes, befitting a powerful and successful man. Elizabeth, in her portrait, is remarkably slender after giving birth to so many children. She holds an object that could either be a snuff box (men and women alike took snuff) or possibly a miniature portrait of her daughter Mary, who had just passed away.

THORNTON, THOMAS GILBERT JR., 12 MAY 1809–2 MAY 1878
ALBERT GALLATIN, 1 FEB 1812–1 SEPT 1891
THOMAS GILBERT, 31 AUG 1769–4 MARCH 1824
SARAH, 20 MARCH 1774–7 NOV 1845

Dr. Thomas Gilbert Thornton was born on August 31, 1769. He married Sarah "Sally" Cutts, daughter of Thomas and Elizabeth Cutts. Their children, born between 1794 and 1816 (just as middle names became popular), were James Brown, Thomas Gilbert, Richard Cutts, Elizabeth Cutts, Sarah Cutts, Mary Cogswell, Anna Payne, Thomas Gilbert, Thomas Gilbert 2nd, Albert Gallatin, Caroline Augusta and Sydney Hamden. (Anna Payne was named for First Lady Dolley Payne Madison's younger sister who married Anna's uncle, Richard Cutts.) Initially, Thomas was a merchant, but he later also became the marshal of Maine. In 1821, when Saco Academy was in danger of bankruptcy, he gave $1,000 to sustain it; it was renamed Thornton Academy in his honor.

A fancy ball at the Thornton home was planned to celebrate the visit of Lafayette to Saco on his grand return tour as an elderly man, but Thomas didn't live to see it. Regardless (John Haley reported), it didn't come off as anticipated. Lafayette ate dinner before arriving. Then neighborhood boys

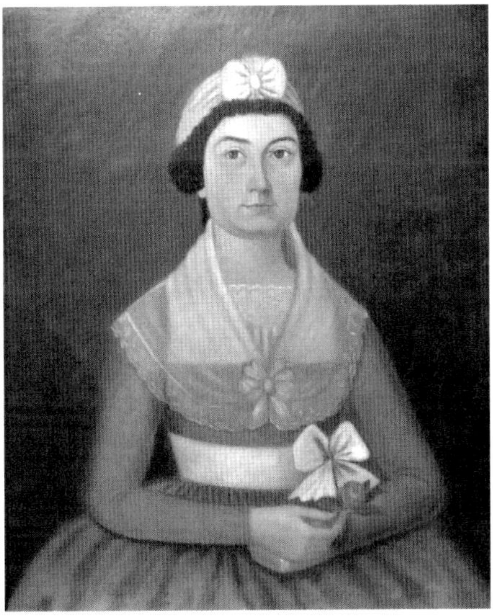

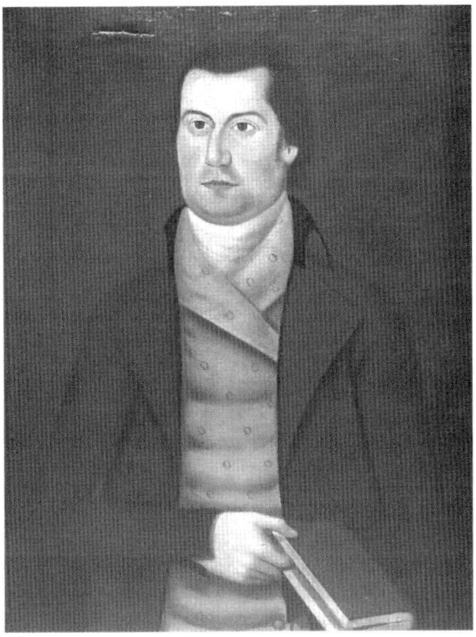

Local artist Charles Henry Granger painted copies of portraits of Thomas Gilbert Thornton and his wife, Sally Cutts, that were originally done by John Brewster Jr. in about 1793. The location of the Brewster portraits is unknown. *Collection of Saco Museum.*

supposedly snuck into the dining room and stole most of the delicacies that'd been prepared for the banquet. Among the thieves were Thomas Gilbert Thornton Jr. (who surely should have known better!), John and Richard Hartley, Joseph Leland and Quin Scamman, all of whom recalled the event with great humor in their later years.

It seems likely that Thomas and Sally aren't buried in this plot—there's a second family plot about one hundred feet to the east that also bears their names. Perhaps the inclusion of their names on this gravestone was in order to provide additional information about the family rather than to mark their graves. Thomas Gilbert Thornton Sr. died long before Laurel Hill was opened and was buried in Pepperrell Park.

ABBOTT, SAMUEL, A.M., D. 8 MAY 1792, AGED 32 YRS.

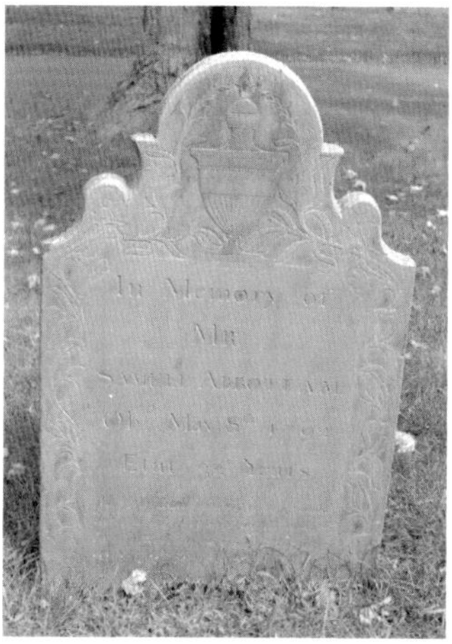

Samuel Abbott's headstone is a marvel of stonecutting artistry. It was moved from the Pepperrell burying ground. *Authors' collection.*

Samuel Abbott has one of the earliest gravestones in Laurel Hill Cemetery. Abbott graduated from Harvard and in 1788 married Mary, the oldest daughter of Thomas and Elizabeth Cutts. They were the parents of two very young sons, Samuel and Thomas, when Samuel died of consumption in 1792. Mary passed away just two years later. On October 26, 1797, Benjamin Simpson wrote in his diary that he was laying bricks for a tomb for Colonel Cutts, Mary's father, in Pepperrell burying ground. Thomas was planning ahead, as he didn't actually die until 1821, but he was probably having the tomb constructed for Mary and Samuel. Two days later, Benjamin wrote, "Took up the remains of Samuel Abbott & his wife & a child of Doct Thornton's [a Cutts grandchild] and deposited them in a tomb of Col. Cutts." Perhaps Samuel had this gravestone placed by the tomb. Whatever the case, when it (and hopefully he) were moved to Laurel Hill, gravediggers put his footstone right next to his headstone. Both of the Abbotts' orphaned sons died rather young. Samuel drowned at New London, Connecticut, in 1813, and Thomas died in 1817.

Samuel's stone was almost certainly carved by Levi Maxcy, who was born in Attleboro, Massachusetts, in 1770 and then worked in Salem from about 1792 to 1811. Later, Maxcy got into serious financial difficulties, and by 1817 or so, he had been jailed for failing to pay his debts. In 1820, he relocated to South Carolina to live near his more financially successful brother. Abbott's stone is strikingly similar to one that Maxcy carved for Ruth Webb at around the same time.

COCHRANE, CLARENCE F., 1901–1944
DR. J.D., 1851–1924
IDA M., 1861–1914

On June 23, 1833, Sally Cochran, who was twenty-eight, went to pick strawberries in the meadow with her husband's farmhand, Abraham Prescott, who was about eighteen. If she was worried that five months before, Abraham had viciously attacked her and her husband, Chauncey, with an axe while they were sleeping, her actions didn't reflect it. Abraham would later offer several explanations as to why he took up a fence post and beat Sally to death in the meadow. He would be tried twice for murder and eventually executed in January 1836.

Shortly thereafter, her husband relocated to faraway Corinth, Maine. Later, he married the daughter of one of the jurors for Abraham's first trial, Maria Gay. He and Maria would become parents to nine children, of whom five survived to adulthood. Jasper D. Cochrane was one of their set of twins. After growing up in Corinth (near Bangor), he left the state, studying at Wesleyan University and then attending medical school in New York City. He returned to Maine and opened a medical practice on Main Street in Saco. In 1899, when he was forty-eight, he married Ida May Hutchins of Fryeburg, Maine, who was then thirty-seven. They had two children. When their son, Chauncey, was born in 1901, Jasper named him either for his father or perhaps for his only dimly remembered older brother who had died young. In 1902, Sarah (who was called "Sally" during her childhood) was born.

A brief biography of Jasper listed his many activities: "He is a member of Corinthian Lodge, No. 59, of Odd Fellows, of East Corinth; Mystic Tie Lodge, No. 7, Knights of Pythias, of Saco; Saco Lodge, No. 9, Free Masons; York Chapter, No. 5, Royal Arch Masons; Main Council, Royal and Select Masters, of Saco; Bradford Commandery, No. 4, Knights Templar; Maine

Conclave, No. 1, Knights of Red Cross of St. Constantine, and also of Kora Temple. He is a life member of the Sons of the American Revolution."

Ida died in 1914. In 1920, Jasper, then sixty-eight, married his English live-in housekeeper, Annie Whitworth, who was thirty years younger. He died four years later. After that, Annie ran a rooming house, assisted off and on by Sally, who never married but who worked in an office throughout the rest of her life. Jasper's son, Chauncey ("Clarence"), became an auto mechanic in Saco. He married Germaine Bonneau and was the father of one son, Jasper D. By 1940, Clarence was divorced and boarding in a rooming house, and Germaine and Jasper had moved in with her father. Clarence died in 1944.

THE CIRCLE AND GREENWOOD AVENUE INTO OAK AVENUE

DAVIS, DANIEL JOSEPH, JR., S2/C. U.S.N., 1922–1942; D. IN ACTION ON BOARD U.S.S. VINCENNES OFF GUADALCANAL, 10 AUG 1942
DANIEL J. SR. 20 MAY 1893–12 FEB 1981
BARBARA JEAN 17 MARCH 1895–21 MAY 1997
THOMAS Q. 25 APR 1919–28 NOV 2012
FLORENCE C. 6 MAY 1920–9 NOV 1997

The USS *Vincennes* was a heavy cruiser that'd been operating in the Pacific theater since mid-April 1942, only four months after the Pearl Harbor attack. On August 7, the *Vincennes* arrived off the coast of Guadalcanal to support landing operations. For a few days, the ship beat off sporadic Japanese air attacks. Just after midnight on August 9, the *Vincennes* went to the aid of two other American vessels that were under attack. Men on the *Vincennes* were unaware that a superior force of five Japanese cruisers and a destroyer had just arrived in the area (although another part of the fleet off Guadalcanal had been warned). Within minutes, the Japanese force began engaging the *Vincennes.* The very first barrage destroyed the bridge, carpenter shop, Battle 2 Station and all radio antennas. Further shelling and then direct strikes by two torpedoes followed. *Vincennes* was now dead in the water and listing heavily. At 2:30 a.m., the captain ordered the crew to abandon ship. They had just minutes to accomplish this, as *Vincennes* rolled over and sank at 2:50 a.m. Seaman Second Class Daniel Davis, just twenty years old, was among the third of the crew that died that night.

The third and youngest child of Daniel Davis, a lineman for the electric company, and his wife, Barbara Jean Quigley, Daniel grew up in Saco and graduated from Thornton Academy in 1941. He was a talented golfer and basketball player—a boy whom his friends described as being lazy in movement and speech, with a slow grin, but a person who got a lot of work done. All of his family is gone now.

TROTTER, THOMAS, 21 NOV 1875–20 APR 1948
KATE M. CHRYSLER, WIFE OF THOMAS TROTTER, 31 MAY 1882–7 JULY 1970
RUFUS W., 22 MAY 1920–3 SEPT 1925
PVT. DAVID HARRISON, CO. E, 112TH INF., 28 DIV., B. 17 JUNE 1922, D. IN VOSSENACK, GERMANY, 4 NOV 1944

David was born in China. His father, Thomas Trotter, from Charlotte, North Carolina, worked for the U.S. government and later for the Saco textile mills. He'd been sent to China in about 1918 to aid with the design of textile mills. While he and his wife, Kate Chrysler (of Hopewell, New York), were there, she gave birth to their three children: Rufus in 1921 (who died in China at the age of five,) David in 1923 and Evelyn Mae in 1926. In the late 1920s, the family returned to the Unites States, and by 1931, they were living on High Street in Saco. David's father worked at the mills, and his mother operated a small dog kennel. David attended schools in Saco and Old Orchard Beach but left school at around the eighth grade and took a job at the Saco Lowell shops. On December 22, 1942, he entered the U.S. Army as a private. After basic training in Texas, he was assigned to Company E, 112th Infantry Regiment, 28th Infantry Division, as a medic.

In late October 1944, the next step toward defeating Germany would involve crossing the Rhine. Standing in the way was a huge, densely wooded area called the Hürtgen Forest. Over the course of the battle to take this woodland, thirty-three thousand Americans would become casualties. On November 2, troops from the 112th were tasked with taking the town of Vossenack. One G.I. would say, "It turned out to be the worst place of any." Sadly, later armchair tacticians would conclude that the objective was worthless; the forest itself could have been bypassed. On November 4, after two days of costly, bloody, freezing fighting, David entered a building in Vossenack. He may have been one of the soldiers of the 112th who took turns seeking refuge there from relentless machinegun and artillery fire—

or perhaps he ran in to care for a wounded man. Whatever the case, the building was hit by artillery and collapsed. Within days, the beleaguered troops would fall back and not regain the ground until much later. David's body was never recovered.

After David's father died, both Evelyn (class of 1948 at Thornton; voted "most bashful" by her classmates) and her mother left Saco, settling in Tacoma, Washington. Kate died in 1970 and was buried with her husband. Evelyn may have married as many as five times. After her mother's death and her own last marriage, she moved to Longview, Texas, where she bought a small home and later moved to a retirement home, where she now lives.

All around the area of the Circle grow white hawthorn trees that blossom in springtime.

Ricker, Alden Hadley, 6 Dec 1848–2 June 1939
Clara Adelaide, 17 July 1867–7 July 1945

Alden Hadley Ricker, the second youngest of seven children, lived all of his long life on the family farm. Until his parents passed away, he lived with them and an unmarried sister in Lyman. He was fifty-nine when he married Clara Adelaide, a thirty-nine-year-old dressmaker. On the 1920 census, they are listed with a fourteen-year-old daughter, but she didn't appear on the 1910 census, so it's possible they had adopted her. The Rickers seem to have led quiet, practical lives, but they chose a very fancy, highly decorative gravestone to mark their graves.

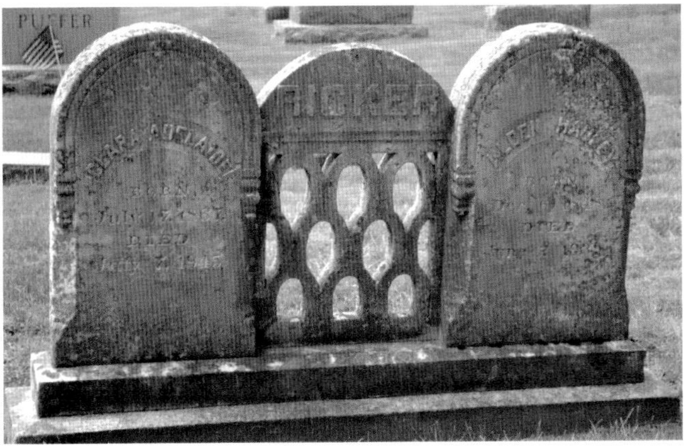

The Ricker headstone is elaborate, attractive and unusual. *Authors' collection.*

Leavitt, George A., 15 Oct 1846–19 Oct 1909
Sarah O., wife of George A. Leavitt, 31 March 1847–29 Dec 1885
Anna E., wife of George A. Leavitt, 29 June 1849–24 Feb 1906
Sarah W., wife of Henry J. Leavitt, 7 Sept 1867–22 Jan 1916
Henry J. 1869–1951
Barbara Ripley, Poetess, 11 June 1914–3 Nov 1939

Barbara's grave is one of only a few in the cemetery with an image of the person on it. She was born in Saco on June 11, 1914, and when she was just a year and a half old, her mother, Sarah, died. In 1919, Henry, a machinist in the Saco Lowell shops and the son of George and Sarah O. Leavitt, married for a second time to Faith Merrill Ripley, who was the divorced daughter of Hampton and Martha Merrill (and twenty years younger than Henry). Two years later, daughter Priscilla was born. At some point, Barbara took Faith's previous married name as a middle name. Barbara graduated from Thornton Academy in 1932. Her classmates said of her, "'Speech is silver; silence is golden.' If that is true, Barbara must be quite rich. She has been so quiet and bashful that we have hardly known her outside of class. She is always quite reticent until she gets paper and pencil. Then her contributions

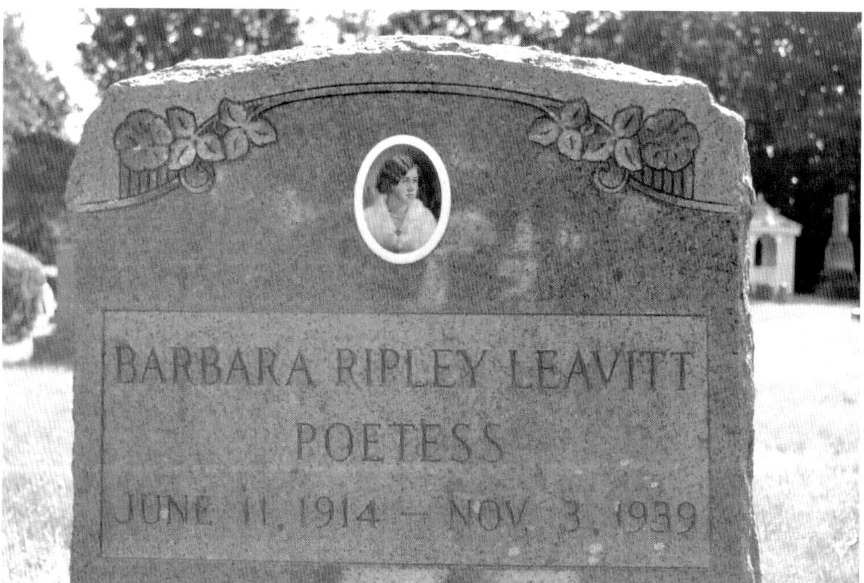

Barbara Ripley Leavitt's headstone is one of only a few that includes a photograph. *Authors' collection.*

to the Tripod are greatly appreciated." Her classmates called her appearance "ladylike" and said that her favorite hobby was reading.

After she graduated from Thornton, she was employed by Pepperrell Manufacturing in its office. She died at the age of twenty-five "after a long illness"—perhaps tuberculosis. Her obituary says that she had had her "poems published in magazines, newspapers and poetical works." "Friendship, The Waltz" bears the copyright of Barbara, who presumably wrote the lyrics.

MAGNOLIA AVENUE

GETCHELL, ANNIE L., 1854–1917
NAHUM [FATHER], 6 JUNE 1814–26 MARCH 1895
JOANN [MOTHER], 30 AUG. 1815–10 JUNE 1897
LEONARD, D. 24 JAN. 1879, AGED 55 YRS., 4 MOS, 14 DAYS
CLARA A., DAU. OF NAHUM AND JOANN GETCHELL, D. 21 SEPT. 1845, AGED 1 YR. 15 DAYS
FRANKLIN N., SON OF NAHUM AND JOANN GETCHELL, D. 4 AUG. 1847, AGED 1 YR. 3 MOS. 7 DAYS
GEORGE F., SON OF NAHUM AND JOANN GETCHELL, D. 20 AUG. 1848 AGED 4 MOS.

Nahum and Leonard Getchell, born in Sanford, Maine, were sons of Jotham Getchell and Ruth Perkins. Nahum relocated to Saco in early adulthood, married Joann Wakefield and found work in the mills. He rose through the ranks rapidly; even in 1850, he was described as a "manufacturer" instead of just a man who "works in cotton mill." Later, he became the overseer—an important and well-paying position. The family lived on Storer Street. Even their relatively well-off status couldn't protect their children from the many diseases that afflicted (and killed) the young. Parenting books of the nineteenth century discuss the perils of "the second summer." Often, by the time a child's second summer came around, the toddler had recently been weaned from the safe diet of breast milk and was now eating table foods and was thus exposed to all of the bacteria that they might harbor in an era before effective

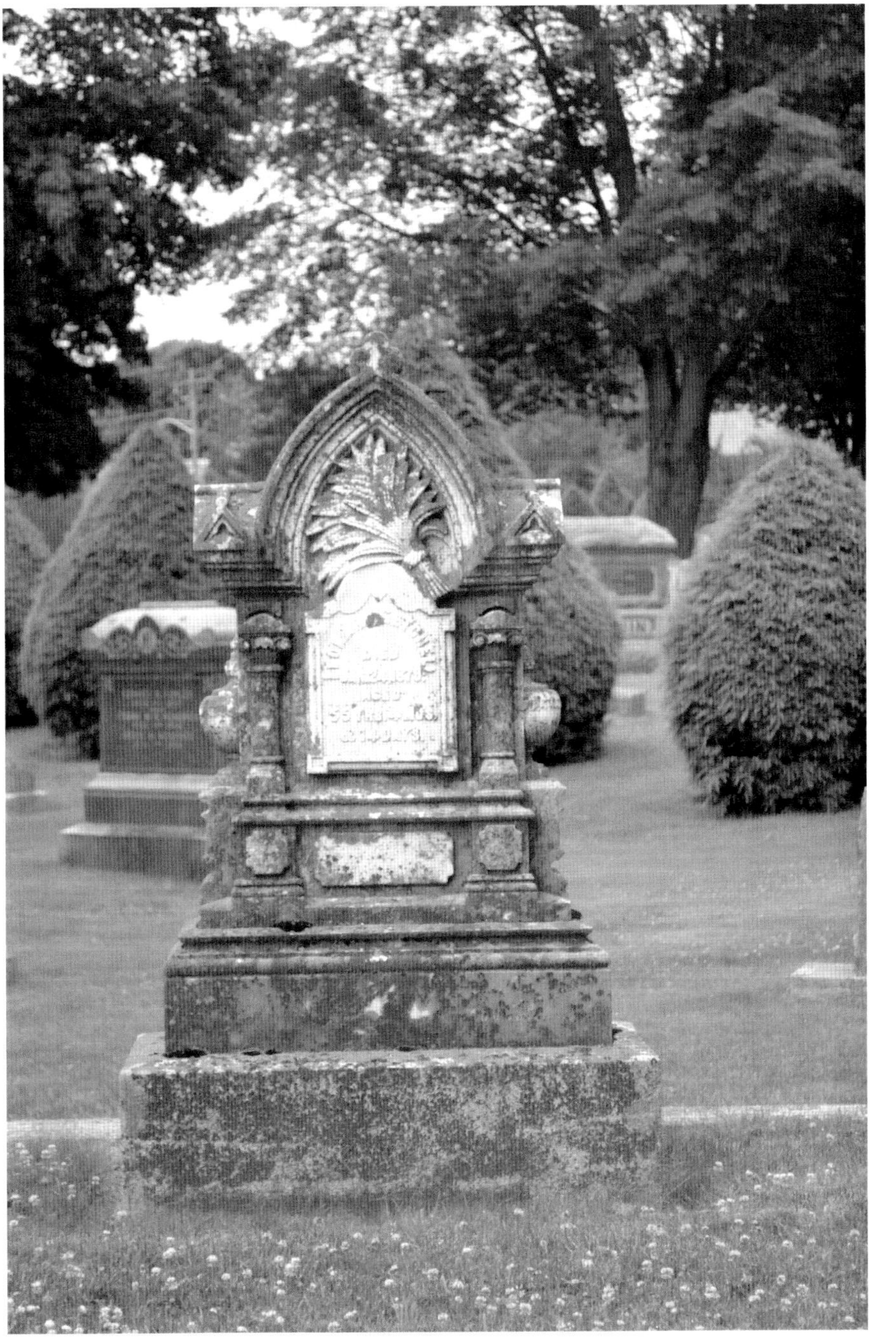

Charles Cleaves carved Leonard Getchell's very decorative headstone. *Authors' collection.*

refrigeration. Perhaps when little George approached the time of year that had already been so lethal for their other children, the Getchells felt relatively safe because it was just his *first* summer. The Getchells were also parents to another son, Charles, born in 1850, and two daughters, Mary and Annie, all of whom lived to adulthood.

Leonard was a full ten years younger than Nahum. He remained on the family farm until his late twenties, working as a teamster. Then he sought his fortune in bustling mill town Lawrence, Massachusetts, before moving to Biddeford for the last few decades of his life, where he worked as a carpenter. Marble worker Charles H. Cleaves signed the bottom of Leonard's large decorative stone. His elaborate grave appears to sit underneath the roof of a gabled house. A sheaf of wheat is sometimes said to symbolize long life—but probably not in the case of Leonard. It can also represent a gift from God or everlasting life (as in the wheat that was used to make the bread consumed at the Last Supper). The complex Gothic font on Nahum and Joann's stones is similar to the writing on the stones of members of Frances Rice's family, also done by the Cleaves shop.

HALEY, JOHN [FATHER], CO. I, 17TH MAINE, 3 MARCH 1840–7 APR. 1921
ABBIE A. [MOTHER], WIFE OF JOHN HALEY, 17 JUNE 1845–5 FEB 1933
ADELAIDE, DAU. OF JOHN AND ABBIE A. HALEY, 16 OCT 1875–15 MARCH 1961
G.E. [HUSBAND], 1877–1964
BATCHELDER, STEPHEN P., D. 21 APR 1867, AGED 67 YRS. 4 MOS.
HANNAH, WIFE OF STEPHEN P. BATCHELDER, D. 29 MAY 1866, AGED 54 YRS. 11 MOS.
CHARLES E., 1 SEPT. 1853–17 JAN 1920
SARAH I., WIFE OF CHARLES E. BATCHELDER, 3 SEPT 1854–29 JAN 1915
DELAND, GEORGE W. 1864–1865

The Haley plot is just behind the Getchell plot. John Haley grew up in Biddeford impoverished—or nearly so—the son of Nathan Haley and Mehitable Barnes Lee. His family, reduced by the early deaths of his three sisters, was a small one, but money was tight enough that he had to leave school at about the age of ten to find work. John's job was to keep the young women who were tending the spinning machines provided with empty spools and to carry away the filled ones. He held the position for seven years before an economic downturn led to the closing of the mill. After nine months of unemployment, Haley found another mill job that he

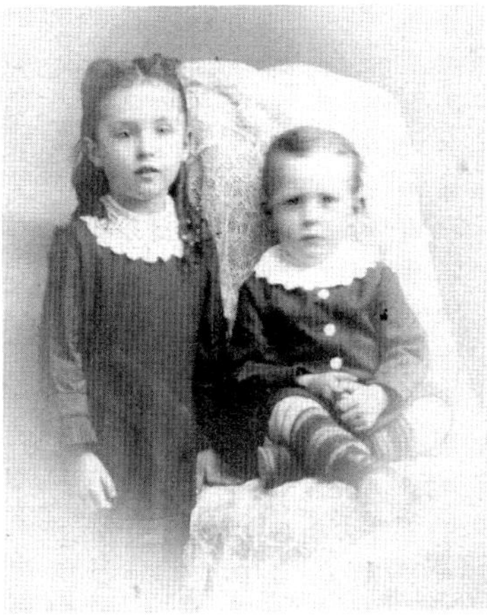

John Haley was a community activist who seems to have rarely (or never) had his own photograph taken, but his two children sat for a picture in about 1880. *Collection of Dyer Library/ Saco Museum.*

held until he enlisted in the Union army with a friend, on a dare.

John became a member of the newly formed Seventeenth Maine Volunteer Regiment, Company I, on August 7, 1862. After a short stint in a Portland camp, he was sent south, first on a brief hot march through Portland and then "packed like sheep" on railroad cars (that were then locked to prevent escape) to Boston, by ship to Maryland and finally by foot and railroad to Washington, D.C. Haley's first battle was a miserable, pointless slaughter at Fredericksburg, Virginia, where Union generals threw their unfortunate soldiers against a well-defended height of land, resulting in absurd and worthless carnage. From there, Haley would go on to fight at nearly every other major battle that occurred in the Eastern theater, finally mustering out on June 19, 1865, three months after the war had ended. As Oliver Wendell Holmes Jr. put it a few years later, "We have shared the incommunicable experience of war. In our youth, our hearts were touched by fire."

Like the rest of the veterans, Haley returned to civilian life still a very young man. He started a career, married and raised children. But like many others, he found the experience of war hard to forget. To deal with his memories, he recorded them in a lengthy diary, probably working from notes he'd taken during his years of service. Since Haley eventually became the long-serving second librarian of the Dyer Library, his beautifully hand-transcribed diaries became part of the Dyer Library collection. Haley kept very busy with Civil War veterans' activities.

He married Abbie A. Batchelder, one of the nine children of Stephen and Hannah Batchelder. Stephen was at various times a ship captain (his primary career) but also worked as a farmer and served as a lighthouse keeper. Little George W. Deland was the son of the Batchelders' eldest daughter, Margaret, and her husband, Francis Deland. Margaret would have six little girls before she died in 1875 but no more sons. John's daughter, Adelaide, never married and taught school. George Edwin Haley worked in the mills and married Nellie Swett, and they adopted a son, Gordon.

KENDRICK, N. FRANK, 1836–1873
ISABELLE L. FOWLER, WIFE OF N. FRANK KENDRICK, 1842–1918
SETH, 1795–1857
SARAH G., WIFE OF SETH KENDRICK, 1799–1868
GEORGE W., 1842–1864, PVT. CO. A, 10TH MAINE VOLUNTEERS
FRANK W.H., 1872–1933
GRACE M., 1874–1956
FOWLER, EDWARD S., 1824–1892

Buried just behind the Haley family is the Kendrick family. Seth Kendrick, half-brother of Clementine Kendrick Burns's father, created a home for his family by salvaging the ell of the Marshal Thornton house when it was to be torn down. Kendrick moved the house to Cross Street. He and Sarah Banks had at least nine children: Rufus, 1820; Mary Jane, 1821; Elizabeth, 1827; Seth, 1830; Sarah, 1832; James, 1834; Noah, 1836; Charles, 1839; and George, 1843. According to John Haley, one night in 1857, one of Seth's sons came home quite drunk. He loudly threatened to kill his father. Seth took refuge under a bed, where he succumbed to his fear—or possibly a heart attack. Presuming the story to be true, it's likely that neither George nor Charles was the guilty son, as they were both still quite young. Rufus had moved out by 1850, leaving Seth, James and Noah as potential culprits. Saco death records only note that Seth died "very suddenly."

Both Seth and George enlisted in the Civil War—George on October 16, 1861. He joined Company A of the Tenth Maine. The Tenth saw very active service, fighting Stonewell Jackson in the Shenandoah Valley Campaign of the summer of 1862 and also taking major roles at Cedar Mountain, Antietam, Chancellorsville and Gettysburg. George survived all those engagements but died of disease on December 30, 1864, only four months before the war would end. Seth didn't enlist until October 4, 1864, in Company M of the Second Regiment Cavalry. He was mustered out in December 1865.

Noah ("N. Frank"), who worked in the cotton mills, married Isabelle Philpot. They were the parents of just one child, Frank W.H., before Noah's early death. Isabelle quickly remarried to another, though much older, cotton mill worker, Edward Fowler, who also died quite soon afterward. After Edward's death, Isabelle lived on with her son. Frank married and divorced and took up farming in Dayton. In 1920, he married Grace Ricker Grant, also divorced. The couple had no children.

GOODWIN, ABBY [MOTHER], WIFE OF NATHANIEL GOODWIN, D. 22 NOV 1858, AGED 68 YRS.

CHARLES E., SON OF LUTHER L. AND MARY E. GOODWIN, KILLED AT THE BATTLE OF THE WILDERNESS, VA., 6 MAY 1864, AGED 24 YRS.

MARY E., WIFE OF LUTHER L. GOODWIN, D. 14 FEB 1891, AGED 77 YRS.

LUTHER L., D. 23 SEPT 1874, AGED 60 YRS. 3 MOS.

HENRY W., SON OF LUTHER L. AND MARY E. GOODWIN, D. SEPT [REMAINDER OF INSCRIPTION BELOW GROUND]

In life, the Goodwin family was a near neighbor of the Getchell family, both living on Storer Street. In death, they are also neighbors. Like Nahum Getchell, Luther Goodwin was an overseer in the mills. Almost certainly Luther was the son of Nathaniel and Abby Goodwin. (It's probable that this is the Nathaniel Goodwin who married Abigail Josephine Berry in Biddeford in 1811.) The births of some of their children are recorded in Biddeford's vital records, but there's no mention of Luther's birth. However, there is a teenager of the right age living in the family on the 1830 census to be Luther. By April 9, 1840, when his son Charles was born, Luther had married Mary Bryant. No record could be found for the birth of their other son, Henry, whose grave had already sunk too far into the ground to have readable dates when *York County Cemetery Inscriptions* was written.

Charles, who first worked as a "journeyman painter" (sort of an apprentice), enlisted in the Union army and was assigned to Company I of the Seventeenth Maine, the same company as John Haley, who noted that Charles was "rheumatic." May 6, 1864, was the second deadly day of the Battle of the Wilderness, a particularly brutal fight that took place in a forest that was thick with dense undergrowth. The Seventeenth was engaged in the heaviest fighting on both days and in severe heat. Especially on the second day, fires started all along the battle line, set off by burning cartridges. Many of the wounded were unable to escape the flames. No one seems to have noted when Charles fell, but he was among the almost unspeakably high 47 percent casualties suffered by the regiment. With his loss, Luther and Mary were now childless. After Luther died in 1874, Mary was able to remain in their home, living off what they had saved.

NORTH AND CENTRAL AVENUES

PERKINS, MAYNARD C., 1874–1970
LAURA BROOKS, WIFE OF MAYNARD C. PERKINS, 1878–1966
ANNIE PAYNE FAIRFIELD, WIFE OF CYRUS MAYNARD PERKINS, 1846–1935
RIPLEY, LUCY PERKINS, DAU. OF CYRUS AND ANNIE PERKINS, 1876–1949
FAIRFIELD, ICHABOD, D. 19 MARCH 1824, AGED 61
SARAH, WIDOW OF ICHABOD FAIRFIELD, D. 22 JUNE 1830, AGED 61
MARTHA A., D. 19 AUG 1838, AGED 34
JOHN, 1847
HAMILTON, BENJAMIN FRANKLIN, SON OF BENJAMIN RICKER AND SARAH CARLE HAMILTON, 1819–1911
SARAH FAIRFIELD, WIFE OF BENJAMIN F. HAMILTON, DAU. OF JOHN AND ANNA PAYNE FAIRFIELD, 1831–1909
JOHN FAIRFIELD, SON OF BENJAMIN F. AND SARAH F. HAMILTON, 1858–1875
THOMAS CARL, SON OF BENJAMIN F. AND SARAH F. HAMILTON, 1862–1881
BENJAMIN FRANKLIN, SON OF BENJAMIN F. AND SARAH F. HAMILTON, 1873–1873
HARRY FAIRFIELD, SON OF BENJAMIN F. AND SARAH F. HAMILTON, 1856–1943
MADELINE FISHER, WIFE OF HARRY FAIRFIELD HAMILTON, 1887–

Books on the nineteenth century provide plenty of biographical information about the accomplished men of the era, but few include information on talented women. Sarah Fairfield Hamilton is one of those overlooked ladies who led a life of consequence. Her father was John Fairfield, who served in the U.S. House of Representatives, was elected twice as governor of Maine

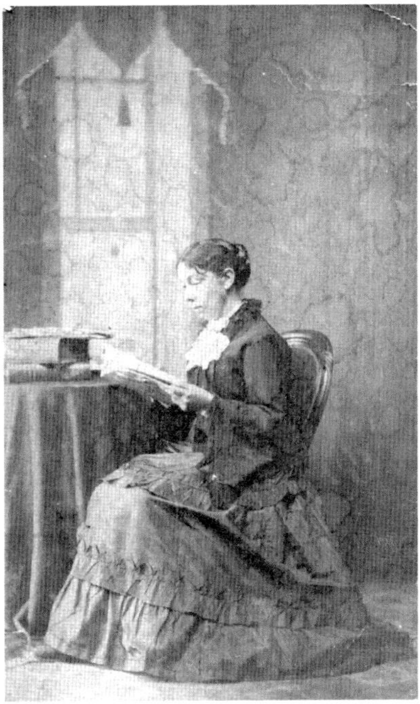

Sarah Fairfield Hamilton was photographed surrounded by books, a reminder of her intellectually stimulating upbringing. *Collection of Dyer Library/Saco Museum.*

and then died from blood poisoning in Washington, D.C., during a term as a U.S. senator after hasty, failed surgery on his knee (before the invention of anesthesia). Born on November 21, 1831, Sarah had four sisters and four brothers (one of whom drowned as a child) and grew up in what must have been a stimulating household. She became active in the community, teaching Sunday school at the Unitarian Church, where she first met her future husband, Benjamin F. Hamilton, who became a Saco merchant. Benjamin operated a "dry and fancy goods" store on Factory Island. After it was destroyed in a fire in 1853, he moved into a new building that was constructed where the old had burned and ran it for the rest of his long career. Benjamin also operated dry goods stores in Biddeford and Portland and ran a blanket mill for a decade. A forward-thinking man, one of his most famous acts was to hire young women to work as clerks in his Saco store in the 1860s. Even though women were working in the mills and some ran their own millinery businesses or taught school, working as a shop girl was viewed as highly inappropriate and many boycotted his store for the first year or so.

Sarah and Benjamin were married in 1853. She gave birth to five sons, ending with a set of twins born on June 19, 1873, one of whom, Benjamin, died the same day. Only Harry, their first born, and Robert, the other twin, lived into adulthood. Sarah remained deeply involved in her community. In about 1881, she traveled to Boston, where she heard women's rights advocate Abby Morton Diaz speak. She spotted Diaz on a streetcar and introduced herself. In response, Diaz came to Saco and encouraged the organization of the first women's club in the area. The club's initial meeting, on March 4, 1882, occurred a full *thirty-eight years* before women in the United States were granted voting rights.

For years, Sarah was the leader of the Saco Women's Educational and Industrial Union. The union raised money by organizing fairs, bazaars and lawn parties, but this wasn't a social club. Many of the same economic issues that troubled the people of Boston could also be found in Saco and Biddeford. The ladies campaigned for sidewalks, began the first area kindergarten and ran it for many years, bought the first playground equipment for the city and were responsible for having home economics classes added to the high school curriculum. Sarah's organization remains active in the twenty-first century.

Sarah is buried with her grandparents, Ichabod and Sarah Nason Fairfield, and the youngest of her siblings, Annie Payne Fairfield, who married Cyrus Maynard Perkins of Kennebunkport (who went by "Maynard"). They immediately relocated to Minnesota Territory, where he worked for the railroad, and she gave birth to at least five children, two of whom were Lucy and Maynard. By 1900, Annie's husband had died, and she had moved with her children to New York City, where her son Maynard became a lawyer, her daughter Ellen was a librarian and her daughter Lucy was a well-known sculptor whose works are still collected.

Ichabod Fairfield's stone was carved by Bartlett Adams in Portland; his widow's was done by Francis Ilsley in the same shop.

COUSENS, JAMES HIRAM, 1845–1910

IVORY W. [FATHER], D. 20 OCT 1904, AGED 85 YRS. 12 DAYS

SARAH A. [MOTHER], WIFE OF IVORY W. COUSENS, D. 10 OCT 1878, AGED 55 YRS. 4 MOS.

RUMERY, ALICE, WIFE OF EDWARD RUMERY JR., D. 23 MAY 1852, AGED 57 YRS.

GEORGE A., SON OF EDWARD AND ALICE RUMERY, DROWNED IN THE SACO RIVER, 27 APR 1842, AGED 10 YRS. 10 MOS., 21 DAYS.

EDWARD, D. 3 DEC 1870, AGED 76 YRS.

ABIGAIL S., WIFE OF EDWARD RUMERY JR., D. 2 MARCH 1870, AGED 72 YRS. 10 MOS.

Edward Rumery was a farmer and a teamster, but he also filled in during the springtime as a gravedigger, helping bury the many dead that had been temporarily stored over the winter (waiting for the ground to thaw) in a tomb at Laurel Hill. Perhaps he got this job because he was the next-door neighbor of sexton Joseph Bradbury. Either way, the tomb had a ventilator on top. According to John Haley, one day Bill King, who was quite the local comedian, came by and saw Edward at his work, lifting a coffin onto his wagon. King crept up on top of the tomb and, using his best scary voice, moaned, "Who art thou that troublest the dead?" Edward, perhaps already feeling a bit edgy, left the tomb at a dead run and was said not to have stopped until he'd reached the safety of his own home. Bill King seems to have enjoyed the joke—no doubt he repeated the story often.

Edward and his first wife, Alice Rose, had just three children. Sadly, their youngest son drowned in the Saco River. The *York Country Democrat* had a full story on the accident:

> *MELANCHOLY LOSS OF LIFE*
>
> *Walter Fairfield, son of the Governor* [Sarah F. Hamilton's brother], *and George Rumery, son of Edward Rumery, both of this town, the former 16 and the latter 12 years of age, were drowned in our river on Wednesday afternoon, by the upsetting of a small punt, which young Fairfield had made with his own hands, and which, though accommodated with a sail, windlass, and other ingenious appurtenances befitting a larger craft, was totally unfit to be trusted beneath any person anxious for his life. At the time of the accident, the boat was at anchor in the swift water immediately opposite Gray's Point—and about a quarter of a mile below the wharves. The two lads, in attempting to haul in their anchor, sank the bow of the boat so as to let in the water; startled at this, in the confusion of the moment, they both ran aft, when the boat capsized, owing in part, probably, to a heavy squall, which swept past at about the same time. The body of young Fairfield was found the same afternoon, and was interred on Friday from the residence of his family. The other body has not yet been found.*

The water temperature in late April would have still been frigid. Hypothermia must have made their situation all the more desperate. The next day's newspaper included an editorial offering condolences—but only to the Fairfield family. It was not noted whether ten-year-old George's body was ever found.

Sarah Rumery Cousens, Ivory's wife and the mother of James Hiram Cousens, was Edward Rumery's sister. The Cousens family lived very modestly in Kennebunk, where Ivory worked as a carpenter. After Sarah died, he remarried but was divorced in 1887. Edward's son James was a confectioner in Kennebunk and never married.

Fairfield, Seth S., 12 March 1790–3 July 1863
Phebee, wife of Seth S. Fairfield, 16 Nov 1797–1 Oct 1859
Jason W., U.S.N., b 27 Nov 1835, d. Pensacola, Fla., 5 Sept 1867
Elizabeth H., dau. of Seth S. and Phebie Fairfield, 8 June 1825–8 March 1844

Born in Wenham, Massachusetts, Seth Fairfield had moved to Saco by 1840. For many years, he worked as a bank cashier. In 1824, he married Phebee Lovejoy, who'd grown up in Conway, New Hampshire. Her older sister, Polly, stayed in the White Mountains and married Samuel Willey Jr. On August 28, 1826, Polly, her husband, their five children (aged four to thirteen) and two hired hands all died in an avalanche in Crawford Notch. Seth and Phebee had one other daughter, Ann, besides the two offspring who are buried with them. On the 1850 census, she was living with her parents in Biddeford. Both Ann and her younger brother, Jason, attended Thornton Academy. She married Gorham Leland of Somerville, Massachusetts. In 1860, Seth was seventy years old and still working at the bank. Late in the spring, he traveled to Boston, perhaps to visit Ann, where he suffered a stroke and died eighteen days later. By 1880, Ann, her husband and three children had moved to Chicago, where she died in 1897. Jason enlisted in the U.S. Navy on November 5, 1862, and served throughout the Civil War as a paymaster. In the summer of 1867, he was most likely stationed at the navy yard in Pensacola, where there was a large postwar federal presence. Early in July, a few cases of yellow fever appeared in the city, but it quickly evolved into a lethal epidemic. Jason was likely among the two hundred or so who died before the disease ran its course in the autumn.

Seth's stone is signed "Adams & Co." This was the gravestone company operated by Arthur H. Adams, born in 1820, and on the 1860 census, he was living with his widowed mother and an unmarried sister and brother in Topsham and described as a "gravestone cutter." His company was listed in the 1856 *Maine Register*. On previous censuses, and on all the ones that followed, Arthur was listed as a farmer, so his company seems to have been somewhat short-lived.

Williams, Capt. William, b. 1814, d. Kennebunk, 22 Nov 1869, aged 55 yrs.
Aphia Storer, wife of Captain William Williams, 4 May 1817–20 Dec 1907
Samuel Storer [Father], 1826–1881

SAMUEL [FATHER], D. 11 NOV. 1874 AGED 90 YRS.
APHIA W. [MOTHER], WIFE OF SAMUEL WILLIAMS, D. 22 JULY 1859, AGED 70 YRS.
WARDROBE, ELIZABETH, DAU. OF SAMUEL AND APHIA STORER, D. 25 MARCH 1850, AGED 18 YRS.
STORER, EUNICE [SISTER], 1812–1879
CHARLES E., [FATHER], 1821–1877
MARIANNA P., WIFE OF CHARLES E. STORER, 1830–1904
WILLIE WILLIAMS, SON OF CHARLES E. AND MARIANNA P. STORER, D. 27 DEC. 1860, AGED 6 YRS. 7 MOS.
CHARLES, JR., 14 OCT 1868–11 JULY 1869
LIZZIE APHIA, DAU. OF CHARLES E. AND MARIANNA P. STORER, D. 4 SEPT 1858, AGED 8 MOS. 14 DAYS
AMOS B., 1856–1881

The Williams clan has a large plot in a prominent location. Captain William Williams was born in England, but by sometime prior to 1850, he had relocated to Saco. That year, he was living in the home of his in-laws, Samuel and Aphia (Woodsum) Storer. Samuel Storer had been born in Wells; his wife was from Saco. Several of their children were born in Biddeford, but in 1850, Samuel was farming in Saco. Later he'd be described as a retired blacksmith. Like many other farmers in Maine, he also carried on a trade, especially in wintertime.

Eunice was Samuel's unmarried sister who lived out her life with him. Among the Storer children, Elizabeth Wardrobe Storer died in her late teens. Samuel Jr. married rather late in life to Ellen Foss and had two daughters before his death in 1881. Charles married Marianna Phelps Boyd from Franklin, Massachusetts, and relocated to West Roxbury, Massachusetts, where he worked as a salesman. Their children—Willie (named for Captain William Williams), Lizzie, Aphia and Charles Jr.—all died quite young. Amos (named for Marianna's father), who was twenty-four on the 1880 census and living with his mother, was an invalid at that point, unable to work due to a lung problem—almost certainly tuberculosis, the highly contagious disease that had killed his father in 1877. Marianna would live on, alone, until she died of a stroke in 1904.

Returning to Captain Williams, a small newspaper article in the *Maine Democrat* from November 30, 1869, reported:

> *Sad Accident About three o'clock Monday afternoon some of the workmen in the lower field of the new ship, building in the yard of Messrs. Crawford*

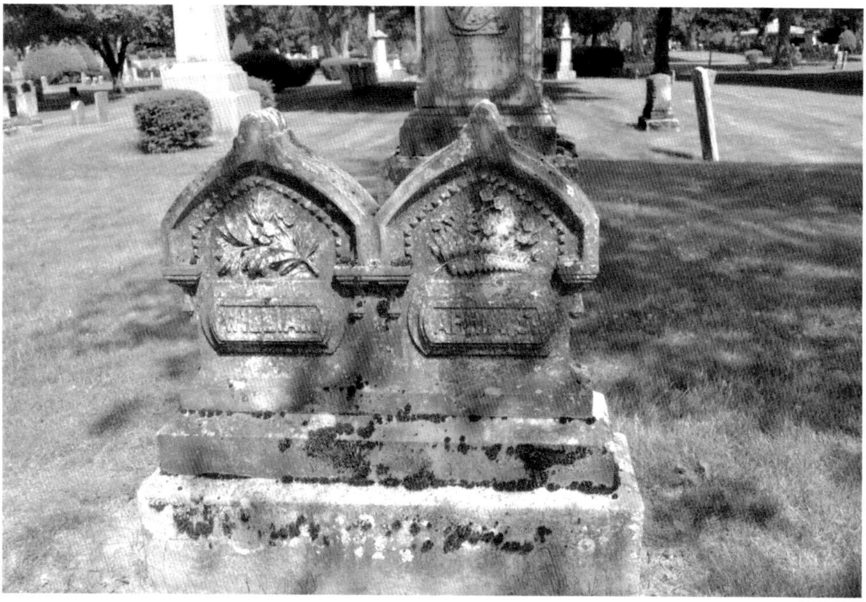

William and Aphia's double stone is decorated by flowers, ferns and an ample growth of lichen. *Authors' collection.*

> *& Ward, Kennebunkport, discovered the body of Captain William Williams, where he had fallen from the lower deck through a small hatch in the afterpart of the ship. He was killed instantly, the back of the head being crushed in. Captain Williams was a native of England, but has resided in Kennebunkport many years, was about fifty five years of age, and had so far superintended the building of the ship where he lost his life. He leaves a wife and a large circle of friends to mourn his untimely death.*

He and Aphia had no children. She never remarried and lived on to the age of ninety, dying of "old age" in Kennebunkport. William and Aphia have both a large urn-topped monument that prominently features an anchor as a symbol of his profession but also share an elaborately carved double gravestone with each side engraved with a different grouping of flowers and foliage.

Skeele, John, d. 2 May 1853, aged 66
Charlotte F., wife of John Skeele, d. 2 Sept 1873, aged 80
Joseph Fessenden, son of John and Charlotte Skeele, d. 25 Aug 1853, aged 19 yrs. 10 mos.
Hannah Brown, 1 May 1829–8 Aug 1901

John Skeele was born in Vermont in 1787 but later moved to Kennebunk, where he married Charlotte Fisher. He was a merchant, operating a hardware and grocery store that also sold goods being imported from the West Indies. Sometime around 1829, when their fourth child and second daughter, Hannah Brown Skeele, was born, the family moved to Sanford. Then, when she was sixteen years old, they relocated to Saco, where John was the secretary of the Mutual Insurance Company. The family lived on Pleasant Street. John died in 1853.

The next time Hannah appeared on a record, it was in St. Louis in 1858, probably drawn there by the presence of her oldest brother, Edwin, who was operating a feed store. She exhibited two drawings at the third annual St. Louis Agricultural and Mechanical Association Fair. The catalogue for the show noted of Hannah, "The artiste must possess great natural aptitude for the art." Throughout the 1860s, she continued to exhibit in St. Louis, usually painting still-life works. One of these was called *Boiled Lobster*—probably not a common subject for a painting in the Midwest at that time! In 1869, she won first place for a painting of fruit. The 1870 census shows Hannah's mother living in a boardinghouse in Kennebunk, unemployed. Perhaps Hannah moved back to Maine around then, although a later newspaper report states that between her time in St. Louis and Maine, she also studied and painted in New York.

Once back in Maine, Hannah became known primarily for her portraits. There are several of her paintings of prominent Kennebunk-area people in the collection of the Brick Store Museum. One of the first she must have done after her return was a postmortem likeness of ten-year-old Lela Perkins, who had died of diphtheria in 1865. Skeele painted throughout the rest of her life, often entering works in local fairs. The 1900 census lists the seventy-one-year-old woman's occupation as "artist." She became ill during the winter of 1900–1901 and passed away in Portland on August 16, 1901. Many of the paintings known to have been done by Skeele are unsigned. There are just sixty-six total works attributed to her, although there are surely numerous others that remain unidentified, especially here in Maine. Hannah accomplished what few other women of her time were able to do:

she became a successful artist, operating in a man's world, selling her work and living on money that she made herself. *Cats* hangs in the Saco Museum, a lovely reminder of Hannah's talent and her clearly gentle hand.

OWEN, [FATHER], 19 AUG 1814–3 FEB 1869
[MOTHER], 17 FEB 1819–29 DEC 1900
LOUISE, DAU. OF WILLIAM H. AND ELLEN OWEN, 26 AUG 1874–29 OCT 1893
WILLIAM H. [FATHER], SON OF DANIEL M. AND MARY J. OWEN, 20 SEPT 1849–24 OCT 1925
MARY B. [MOTHER], DAU. OF ROBERT AND MARY CAMPBELL, 11 JAN 1857–15 MARCH 1933
RICHARD C., SON OF W.H. AND MARY B. OWEN, A.E.F., MED. DEPT. 315TH INF., 79TH DIV., KILLED IN ACTION, 17 NOV 1895–26 SEPT 1918

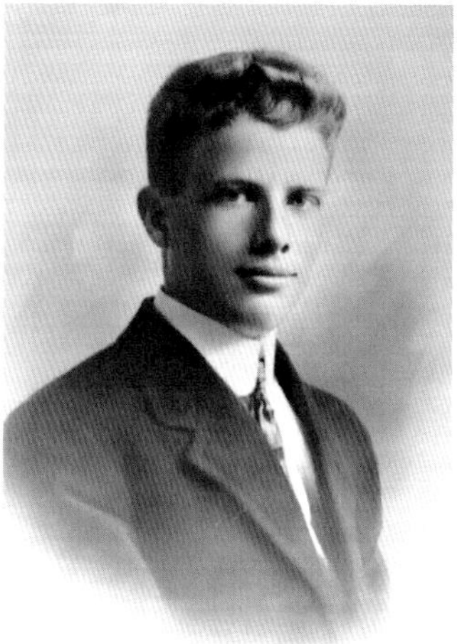

Richard Owen dreamed of becoming a dentist until service as a medic in World War I ended his life. *Collection of Dyer Library/Saco Museum.*

William H. Owen was the son of a tailor, so it's not surprising that he and his brother George both took up the trade. That career may not fully have been to William's liking, though. By the 1890s, city directories reported that he was now a farmer on Beach Street in Saco. After his wife, Ellen Littlefield, and his only daughter, Louise, both died from consumption in 1892 and 1893, he remarried to Mary B. Owen, a "tailoress" who was the daughter of a Scottish immigrant in Biddeford. They had two sons: Henry, born in 1894, and Richard, just a year later.

Richard attended Thornton Academy and was a good student. When he registered for the draft in World War I, he described himself as a short, slender, blue-eyed, brown-haired student at Tufts Dental School. By July 1918, he was traveling to France as a medic in the 315th Infantry, part of the American Expeditionary Force that would quickly tip the balance enough to end World War I. The 315th—all green troops—was sent in several hours after the assault began toward German trenches on the first day of the Battle of the Argonne Forest. Nine men from the 315th died on that first day. One of them was twenty-two-year-old Richard. Later, the Saco American Legion would name its post for Richard Campbell Owen. His older brother became a newspaper reporter. When his first son was born in March 1918, Henry named him Richard C. Owen. That Richard would serve for most of World War II and, fortunately, survive.

Wentworth, Arthur F., 1840–1912
Lucy J., wife of Arthur Wentworth, 1852–1899
George W., son of Asa and Eliza Wentworth, 1838–15 Oct 1852, aged 14 yrs. 9 mos.
Frederick S., son of Asa and Eliza Wentworth, 1848–1 March 1850. Aged 1 yr. 5 mos.
Mary E., dau. of Asa and Eliza Wentworth, 1845–18 Jan 1850, aged 4 yrs. 8 mos.
Asa Dow, son of Asa and Eliza Wentworth, 1843–9 Aug 1844, aged 9 mos. 9 days
Asa, 1814–18 Feb 1877, aged 62 yrs. 5 mos.
Eliza, wife of Asa Wentworth, 1816–15 March 1866, aged 51 yrs. 6 mos.
Shea, Frances J., wife of John Shea, dau. of Asa and Eliza Wentworth, d. 3 Jan 1874, Aged 32 yrs. 6 mos.
Charles, son of John and Frances J. Shea, d. 5 Dec 1874, aged 1 yr. 8 mos.
Baston, Nellie F., dau. of Winthrop and Hattie E. Baston, 5 Jan 1885–5 July 1907

Asa Wentworth, the son of Spencer Wentworth of Wakefield, New Hampshire, was a hardworking man. When he married Eliza Emerson in 1837, they were both living in Lowell, Massachusetts, where he got his start in business. From there, he went on to operate a tavern and hotel, first in Manchester and then in Jaynesville, New Hampshire. Neither of these seems to have returned any profit, and at one point he was briefly jailed for selling liquor without a license. By 1849, he was running the Saco House, a large hotel, on Main Street. He and Eliza had at least seven children: Frederick and Mary, who died in 1850; George, who died in 1852; Asa, who died in 1844; Hattie, who married Winthrop Baston; Arthur, who was living at home in 1860 and helping run the hotel; and Frances, who was also living at home in 1860, working as a merchant with a net worth of $1,000 and who would marry John Shea. In the 1849 *Saco City Directory*, Asa's Saco House employees included Stephen, Henry and John Wentworth; Henry was his younger brother. By 1870, Asa was running a Saco grocery store at 114 Main Street and living on Cross Street, but Eliza was dead. He had remarried to a young woman, Maria, from Nova Scotia. He'd amassed a sizeable estate of $10,000 before he died in 1877, but considering that he owned upward of eighty tenements around that time, this seems like a modest figure.

In an odd footnote to Asa's life, in 1845 a man named Jonas Longley Parker, a tax collector from Manchester, New Hampshire, was waylaid one cold night on his way home from a tavern. Several people heard his screams as he was being attacked in some woods but failed to go to his assistance. Parker's body, with his head nearly severed and both a razor and an odd sharpened shoemaker's knife left by his side, was discovered the next morning. Although a wallet with a very large amount of money was found in his coat, a second one with thousands of dollars more (a small fortune for the time) was missing. Suspicion later fell on Henry Wentworth. Some claimed that he'd been seen in the vicinity, looking pale, late on the night of the crime, and two people (much later) overheard Eliza say that she knew more about it than she was admitting—at the time she said that, though, she was furious with Asa for hosting a late-night gambling party and seemed to be trying to punish him.

There was little (or perhaps *no*) direct evidence to connect Asa and Henry to the crime, but by February 1849, with the murder still unsolved, Henry was charged in Saco with murder and Asa and Eliza with being accessories. After they'd been jailed a while, the magistrate found that there was insufficient evidence to send the Wentworths to Manchester for trial, so they were released. The following year, the governor of New Hampshire demanded that a warrant be issued for Asa, Henry and two men from Lowell, Massachusetts, (where the victim had been born), one of whom was also a Wentworth. This warrant was served immediately after Asa and Eliza had lost two of their younger children, Mary at age four in January and one-year-old Frederick in March. Among their defense attorneys were Franklin Pierce, who would later serve as the fourteenth president of the United States (1853–57), and Benjamin Butler, who would attain infamy as a Civil War Union general. After a month-long preliminary hearing that drew large crowds, the judge ruled that there wasn't enough evidence to hold the two Lowell men, but Asa and Henry were bound over for the grand jury and held in jail. That fall, the grand jury finally also concluded that there wasn't sufficient evidence against them, and charges were dropped. Apparently, however, suspicion against the men remained in Saco primarily because they seemed to have come into unexpected money.

John Haley reported that when "old Dr. Stevens" lay dying, Wentworths hovered around his bedside fearing that he'd make a deathbed confession of whatever he knew about their relatives' role in the murder—which Dr. Elbridge G. Stevens of Biddeford (but born in Lowell) didn't. More than thirty years later, Benjamin Butler mentioned in passing to a friend (and later supposedly detailed in a letter to some Saco Wentworths) that around the time Asa and Henry were being tried in Manchester, he was also representing a man named Daniel H. Pearson (or Pierson) who was accused of murdering his wife, Martha, and twin daughters, Sarah and Lydia, with a razor and an odd sharpened shoemaker's knife and then leaving the weapons at Martha's side. Pearson was known to hold a grudge against murder victim Parker as well. According to Butler, while Pearson was awaiting execution for killing his family, he "all but" confessed to murdering Parker. Butler had no explanation for why he waited so very long to reveal this telling evidence that someone else had murdered Parker, not his clients. No one else was ever charged with the crime.

Rice, Henry Jay, 1816–1894
Melinda B., 1823–1909
Philip Henry, son of Henry J. and Melinda B. Rice, d. 8 Dec 1876, aged 19 yrs. 6 mos.
William B., 1844–1923
Frank C., 1841–1929
Edith Marion, 3 Apr 1861–10 Feb 1933
Elizabeth, 14 Feb 1855–1 Oct 1937.
"Established a generous fund in memory of her father Henry J. Rice and her brother Frank C. Rice which is to be used that this cemetery shall forever remain a place of beauty."

Elizabeth can be credited for much of the current appearance of Laurel Hill Cemetery, as her very large gift led to its reworking and revitalization beginning in the 1930s. Elizabeth was among the children of Henry J. Rice and his wife, Melinda. In his younger years, Henry was a moderately successful merchant. By the time he was in his sixties, when he was asked what he did for a living, he said he had "never had a business," an adamant (and unusual) response, noted by the census taker. After he died in 1894, Elizabeth and

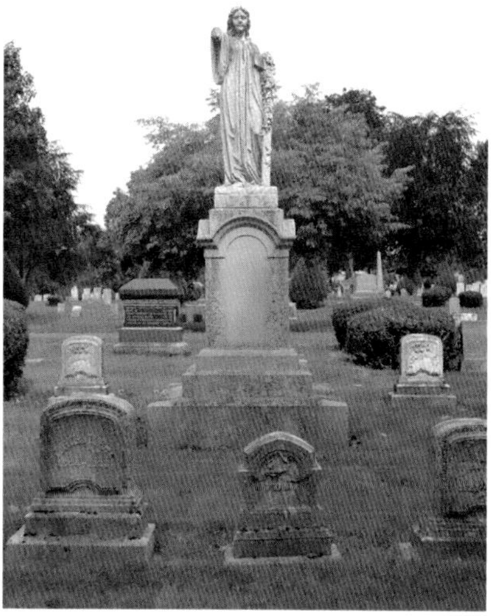

Elizabeth Rice had her family plot decorated with expensive Cleaves markers and an angel. She gave most of the rest of her estate to the cemetery. *Authors' collection.*

her younger sister, Edith, continued to live in the family home on High Street with their older brother William ("Willis"), who worked as a carriage painter. This painstaking work not only included applying the base colors to carriages but also adding the fine paint details that required artistry and a steady hand—highly skilled work. In the last years of his life, when he was in his seventies and cars had replaced carriages and his occupation had become obsolete, he resorted to working in the cotton mill.

Elizabeth and Edith never seem to have held paying jobs. Frank left Maine in young adulthood; relocated to Quincy, Massachusetts; and married Josephine of Eastport, Maine, who died only a few years later. He stayed in the Boston area for the rest of his life, living in boardinghouses and working as a clerk, into his seventies. Even though Elizabeth lived with and depended on Willis until his death in 1923, it was her brother Frank and her father whom Elizabeth memorialized with her gift. Since there doesn't ever appear to have been a large amount of money in the family, all three of the surviving Saco Rices must just have lived very frugally in order to save the funds that became her bequest to the cemetery. The Rice plot includes a large, elaborate Cleaves angel (with a broken arm) and unusual matching stones with Gothic font and raised ridges on the front surface that also came from the Cleaves shop.

LOCUST AVENUE

MESERVE, GEORGE H., 25 JULY 1829–23 OCT 1899
MARY E., 22 MAY 1831–26 SEPT 1915
FRANKIE H., SON OF GEORGE H. AND MARY E., D. 13 MARCH 1863, AGED 1 YR. 4 MOS.
MRS. CAROLINE, WIFE OF CAPT. LUKE MESERVE, D. 2 OCT 1830, AGED 27 YRS.
CHADBOURNE, FRANK, 1859–1920
NELLIE M. MESERVE, WIFE OF FRANK CHADBOURNE, 1860–1930

Frankie H. Meserve was the infant son of George H. and Mary E. Meserve. His grave features a stone carving of a sleeping (or deceased) infant. Sometimes young children's gravestones would have a carved sleeping lamb on top instead. These gentle images stand in sharp contrast to the death's head gravestones that were typical only sixty or seventy years before. George

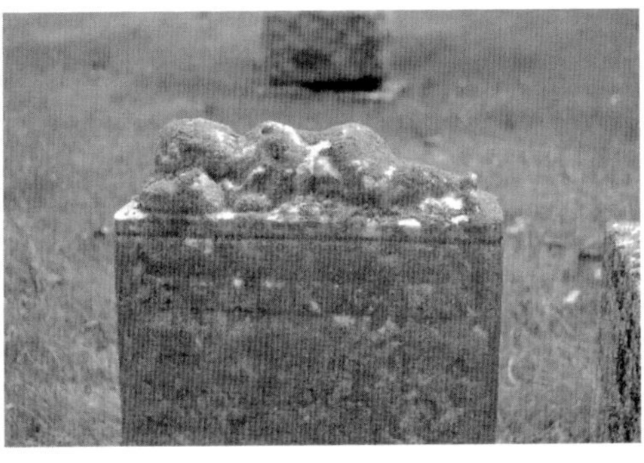

Tiny Frankie Meserve sleeps quietly under a bright blanket of lichen. *Authors' collection.*

Meserve worked as a machinist. He and his wife had at least one other child, Nellie, who was born in 1860 and is buried here with her husband. Captain Luke Meserve was George's brother who died in 1855 in "Canada East" and was buried there. Caroline's slate gravestone is located a small distance away from the rest, across the lane and in an open area. It was very likely carved in the Timothy Eastman shop (as were the Low stones), since it bears such a strong resemblance to other stones done there.

OSBORN, AUGUSTUS KIMBALL, ONLY SON OF AUGUSTUS AND ISABELLA E. OSBORN, SACO, 25 APR 1865–SOMERVILLE, MASS., 26 AUG 1885
WILLIAM P., 6 OCT 1802–5 JULY 1878
ELIZABETH, WIFE OF WILLIAM P. OSBORN, 10 JAN 1833–29 JAN 1907
THOMAS, SON OF WILLIAM AND ELIZABETH OSBORN, D. 9 SEPT 1848 AGED 1 YR. 6 MOS.
HENRIETTA, DAU. OF WILLIAM AND ELIZABETH OSBORN, D. [REST ILLEGIBLE]
ALBERT H., SON OF WILLIAM AND ELIZABETH OSBORN, D. 5 APR 1859, AGED 10 YRS.

William P. Osborn, born in Massachusetts, was a resident of Saco by the time his first child, Dorcas Ellen, was born in 1828—just a week after he married Betsey M. Jackson in Portland. Betsey mothered five children overall, but she and two of her offspring were dead by 1838. In February 1845, William married for a second time, to Elizabeth March—the daughter of Fortune and Violet March of Shapleigh—who may have been as young as twelve when they were wed. On the 1850 census, William was working as a barber. At the time, his was the only black family in all of Biddeford and Saco. He would continue as a barber for most of his life, residing in one half of a Storer Street house. He and Elizabeth would have five children between 1846 and 1853, but it seems likely that none reached adulthood. Their experiences in Saco must have differed in many ways from that of their neighbors. When their information was included in any vital records, their race ("colored") was always added to the notation, lest anyone forget their "different" status. But when William died in 1878, he was buried in a Laurel Hill plot that's indistinguishable from those of other Saco businessmen.

Cleaves, John, d. 1 May 1861, aged 44 yrs. 2 mos.
Jane S., wife of Paul R. Cleaves, d. 25 Aug 1858, aged 54 yrs.
Abigail, wife of Eleazer Cleaves, d. 23 Feb 1833, aged 42 yrs. 10 mos.
Charles E., 1842–1842
Ann, 1820–1862
Harrison, 1815–1874
Charles H., 1847–1917
[illegible], dau. of E. and A. Cleaves, d. 12 July 1832, aged 2 yrs. 5 mos.
Chamberlain, Almira C. Bowdoin, b. 11 June 1825, m. John Cleaves, 14 Jan 1847, m. S.B. Chamberlain, 26 May 1864, d. 6 March 1869

In March 1814, in Harpswell, Maine, Ebenezer "Eleazer" Cleaves of Saco (the son of Ebenezer Cleaves, born in Beverly, Massachusetts, and Abigail Young of Biddeford) married Abigail Cleaves, daughter of Harrison Cleaves and Jane Randall (and also his first cousin). Their children were Harrison (1815), John (1817), Charles (1818), Samuel (1820), Elbridge (1822), Susan Jane (1824), Robert (1827) and the daughter born in 1830 whose name was never recorded in Saco records. With her gravestone now unreadable, her name seems likely lost forever.

In 1847, John married Almira (who remarried after John's early death, although she didn't outlive him by many years). By 1850, John was working in the marble trade with his older brother, Harrison. Harrison would continue working marble for the rest of his life. He married Ann Leighton, and they had two children before her death in 1862 but only one survived: Charles Harrison Cleaves. Charles took up stone carving as well, but only after trying his hand at work in a machine shop and a water power shop for a few years.

In 1872, Charles spent a year in Philadelphia working for sculptor Alexander Milne Calder. Calder was responsible for creating models for the architectural sculptures at the Philadelphia City Hall, a project he began about the time that Charles was working for him. All the large marble sculptures in Laurel Hill Cemetery are believed to have come from the Cleaves shop, and surely many of the plainer stones did too. In addition, one smaller figure on a plinth in Biddeford's Greenwood Cemetery is signed "Harrison Cleaves and Son." Presumably, that stone must date from about 1873–74 since Harrison died in 1874. It may represent the first of Charles's major artistic works. It seems remarkable that the Cleaves family marked their own members' graves with simple stones that, in many cases, don't even include exact birth and death dates or the ages of the people buried there.

Paul R. Cleaves was Eleazer's brother-in-law. He and his wife, Jane, were likely the parents of little Charles E., who was born and died in 1842.

NEW AVENUE

CHASE, CAPT. WILLIAM, SON OF CAPT. WILLIAM AND ALICE CHASE, D. 24 FEB 1882, AGED 75 YRS. 8 MOS.

CAPT. WILLIAM, D. 28 JULY 1817, AGED 42 YRS. 9 MOS.

ALICE, WIFE OF CAPT. WILLIAM CHASE, D. 20 AUG 1876, AGED 95 YRS. 3 MOS. 7 DAYS.

JOHNSON, ALMIRA CHASE, WIFE OF JOHN JOHNSON, D. 4 JAN 1879, AGED 69 YRS. 1 MO.

FRANK CHASE, SON OF JOHN AND ALMIRA C. JOHNSON, D. 18 JUNE 1883, AGED 33 YRS. 3 MOS.

ANNIE C., DAU. OF JOHN AND ALMIRA JOHNSON, 11 SEPT 1846–15 OCT 1926

GLOVER, MARY, B. LONDON, ENGLAND, 10 MARCH 1830, D. SACO, ME., 17 OCT 1907

Captain William Chase Sr. was the son of Samuel and Hannah Chase. William's name appears twice in the death records for Saco, the first time in 1816 when, as captain of the brig *Hazard*, he reported the death of seaman Thomas Kimball. The following year, it was Captain William's death that was noted. His epitaph is appropriate for a sea captain: "My bark is wafted to the strand/By breath Divine/And on the helm there rests a hand/Other than mine."

His widow, Alice Spofford Chase, would live on for almost six more decades before dying at the age of ninety-five. She was the mother of three children: William Jr., Harriet and Almira, born between 1806 and 1809.

William Jr. also went to sea. There appears to be a death notice for him as well: "William, the son of the widow of Captain William Chase Lost at Sea August 27, 1827" is recorded in Saco vital records. It's recorded after deaths that occurred in September and early October, so it was likely entered in the record book when word of his death finally reached Saco. Alice Chase appears to be the only person who was living in Saco in 1827 who would have been described as "the widow of Captain William Chase." Not surprisingly, the 1827 death report has been picked up by many genealogists. But the presence of William Chase, retired master mariner, living in the Biddeford House (a very large rooming house) in 1870, as well as the information on his gravestone, clearly contradicts his death in 1827. It's likely that word reached Saco of his death at sea and that the death was duly recorded, but then William, quite alive, came home—something not all that uncommon at the time. William Chase Jr. seems never to have married. By 1880, he had relocated to a Dover, New Hampshire boardinghouse, where he died of paralysis in 1882.

John Johnson was born in Saco to William Short Johnson and Adah Chase. Adah was one of Captain William Chase Sr.'s sisters. Not long afterward, the Johnson family relocated to Pembroke, New Hampshire, but kept Saco ties, as John later married Almira Chase of Saco. The young couple relocated to New York City, where John played a key role in the design and manufacture of the first camera made in America. Having seen a drawing of the camera just created by Louis Daguerre in France, Johnson enlisted the aid of a friend, Alexander S. Wolcott. The pair patented their creation on May 8, 1840. Not long afterward, William Johnson (and perhaps John as well) traveled to England, where they made huge strides toward improving the material that was painted onto the plates that would be exposed to light in the camera. The result was that exposure time fell sharply from many minutes to just a matter of seconds. Wolcott died in 1844, but neither he nor Johnson ever reaped significant financial benefits from their inventions, even though within just a year or so, photographic studios cropped up in cities and towns all across the country.

Sometime after 1860, Johnson and his family moved back to Saco, where they rented a home at 10 Beach Street. He became one of the founding members of the York Institute (now Saco Museum). A second version of his groundbreaking camera is in the museum's collection—the oldest camera in America. When John Johnson applied for a passport in 1851, he was described as having dark eyes, a prominent nose, a common mouth, a round thin face with thinning auburn hair and a fair complexion. John and Almira's son Frank was a machinist at the Saco Lowell shops. Their daughter Annie never held a job, never married and lived out the rest of her life in the family home, sharing it with Mary Glover until she died. Mary was listed on the 1860 census as being John Johnson's sister, although her different last name and birth in England seem to contradict that she was his birth sister. She lived with the family from at least 1850, when she was just twenty, until her death in 1907 of "acute indigestion." At that time, even Annie was unable to provide the names of Mary's parents.

CHASE, AMOS. "SACRED TO THE MEMORY OF THE VENERABLE AND EMINENTLY PIOUS DEACON." AMOS CHASE, 15 JAN 1718–2 MARCH 1818, AGED 100 YEARS
SARAH COLE, WIFE OF DEACON AMOS CHASE, D. 4 FEB 1781, AGED 56 YEARS
MR. DANIEL, 28 AUG 1762–1 SEPT 1827, AGED 65 YEARS
ELIZABETH, RELICT OF DANIEL CHASE, D. AFTER ILLNESS OF 18 HOURS, 26 JUNE 1834, AGED 69

Behind the William Chase plot are the graves of older Chases, one of whom is the man with the earliest known birth date for Laurel Hill. Amos Chase was born in Newbury, Massachusetts, second among at least nine children of Samuell Chase and Hannah Emery. In about 1734, he moved to Saco, built an "ordinary" (or small inn) on the Saco River and for several years operated the ferry that crossed to Biddeford. Early in his Saco stay, he married Sarah, the daughter of Samuel Cole. In 1741, he and several others attempted to settle Buxton, clearing land and building some cabins. Trouble with Native Americans flared up in 1744, and all of the settlers fled from the Buxton wilderness. Amos and his young family lived in Newbury until peace returned in 1748. They then came back to Saco, operated the ferry for a few more years and finally moved to a home a few miles farther inland, where Amos remained for the rest of his long life. In his later years, he was known for his very long, flowing white hair. He was the long-serving second deacon of First Parish Congregational Church. He was also a member of the Commissioners of Correspondence and Safety, responsible for seeing to it that Saco citizens supported the American cause during the Revolutionary War. He and Sarah are believed to have been the parents of fourteen children, but only their son Daniel is buried with them. Daniel's wife, Elizabeth, who died suddenly, was a daughter of a longtime minister in Manchester, Massachusetts, Reverend Benjamin Toppan (or Tappan) and his wife, Elizabeth March.

HARRIET P. BRADBURY
21 MARCH 1863–10 JUNE 1938

Harriet P. "Hattie" Bradbury was the middle child of the three offspring of mason Edward Bradbury and his wife, Harriet Noble Bradbury. When her older sister, Lizzie, died at the age of eighteen, it left just Hattie and her older brother, Francis, called "Frank." Just after the 1900 census was taken, Hattie's father died. Neither sibling ever married, but they continued to live together, eventually moving into a large home on Main Street just across from the Deering mansion (which would in time become the home of the Dyer Library). Hattie, well supported by Frank, never needed to take a job.

In 1938, she was seventy-five years old and in declining health. On Wednesday, May 9, two boys passed by the house and saw Hattie lying on the porch and crying out in pain. With Frank's help, they carried her inside to a chair and then offered to call a doctor. But Frank said that she'd be okay—in spite of the fact that she appeared to have a broken leg and a head injury. Friday, with the story of her accident around town and with no one having seen her since, the police came by to check on her and found a bloodstained chair and a path of blood leading across the room and down the cellar stairs. There was no sign of Hattie.

When questioned by police, at one point Frank said, "Ask me no questions and I'll tell you no lies." Eventually, he admitted that he'd found her dead in the chair (where he'd left her alone) early on Thursday morning. Not wanting to waste money on a funeral, he dragged her down to the cellar, kindled a hot fire in his furnace and pushed the upper half of her body in, suspending the rest of it with ropes until the first part was cremated and then gradually feeding in the remainder. He was arrested and charged with unlawful disposal of a body. After spending some weeks in Augusta having his sanity evaluated, he was tried the following May, found guilty and sentenced to sixty days in the county jail. Upon his release, he went back to living quietly, although his *extreme* frugality remained a topic of discussion around town until years after his death at home on January 12, 1942. His arrangements were conducted by a funeral director, but he has no stone in Laurel Hill to mark his grave.

PATTERSON, ROGER P., PVT., 7TH [--?] VOL., D. AT [GULANGES?] 28 DEC 1861, AGED 17 YRS. 8 MOS.
HANSEN, DANIEL, 1913–1918
PETER, 1887–1919
SEAVEY, JEDEDIAH F. [FATHER], 18 APR 1825–25 APR 1907
OLIVE J. [MOTHER], WIFE OF JEDEDIAH SEAVEY, 5 SEPT 1834–30 APR 1924
SOLOMON B., D. 23 NOV 1873, AGED 75 YRS. 6 MOS.
BETSEY B., WIFE OF SOLOMON B. SEAVEY, 19 FEB. 1889, AGED 87 YRS., 8 MOS. 19 DAYS
OLIVER, INFANT SON OF SOLOMON B. AND BETSEY SEAVEY, D. 3 AUG 1810
ALONZO, SON OF SOLOMON B. AND BETSEY SEAVEY, D. 21 MAY 1816 AGED 2 MOS.
ALONZO T., SON OF JEDEDIAH AND OLIVE SEAVEY, 1855–1886
SADIE E., DAU. OF JEDEDIAH AND OLIVE J. SEAVEY, D. 19 NOV 1881, AGED 13 YRS. 8 MOS.
[SEAVEY] BABY

Like Orlando and Caleb Hooper, Roger Patterson didn't live long after he enlisted in the Union army. Roger's life, however, represents several mysteries. He was the son of Lydia Milliken and her husband, Roger Patterson, whom she married on October 30, 1845, in Portland. Perhaps her husband soon died. By 1850, Lydia was living with her father and stepmother, Alexander and Sophia Milliken, in Portland, along with her two young children, Rosella (three) and Roger (just one). That would place Roger's birthdate at about 1849. In 1864, when Lydia died in Massachusetts (of "small pox," according to the handwritten record), she was a widow. In 1860, young Roger, aged eleven, was living in Saco with Solomon Seavey and his wife, Betsey Stuart. Roger's relationship to the Seaveys isn't clear.

A Maine adjutant general report indicates that Roger enlisted from Saco in the Seventh Battery of the Maine Light Artillery on November 29, 1864, but his name wasn't included on any official rosters. A Dyer Library record reported that he died on March 6, 1865. (No other record confirmed that death date.) However, according to *York County Cemetery Inscriptions*, his gravestone states that he died at "Gulanges" (actually, this appears to be a different name that's followed by the word "Hospital") on December 28, 1861, at the age of "17 yrs., 8 mos." That would place his birthdate as about May 1844—quite far off from the one indicated by census records. Roger is buried in the family plot of Solomon Seavey, giving solid evidence that he is the same Roger who was living with the family and aged just eleven in July 1860. His age on his gravestone actually appears to be *15* years, 8 months.

The National Archives in Washington, D.C., provided more information. When Roger enlisted on November 29, 1864, his grandfather Alexander Milliken swore an affidavit that the boy was over eighteen years of age, although he surely knew that his grandson (who was just five-foot-two at that time) was far younger. It's been estimated that about 20 percent of Civil War soldiers may have been under the required age of eighteen when they enlisted. Roger's case seems worse because his grandfather was a willing participant in the deceit and because the boy was still very far from eighteen. Tragically, Roger—who, like many farm boys of the era, had been exposed to few contagious diseases—got sick with measles within just a week or two of enlisting. He was sent to Gallops Island, a tiny outpost in Boston Harbor, where the Union army operated a training camp and hospital. In the midst of winter, it must have been wind-whipped and brutally cold. On December 28, 1864, the boy died. His meager belongings—most of them government issued but also including a testament, a "pocketbook" or wallet and a memorandum book (probably intended to become a diary)—were auctioned. The money raised, a little over nine dollars, and Roger's body were returned to Maine. Roger's gravestone toppled over a long time ago.

Solomon Seavey was a farmer on Flag Pond Road. Besides two children who died as infants, he and Betsey were parents to at least nine others, including Jedediah. Peter Hanson, buried next to Roger, was born in Norway and worked as a machinist at the Saco Lowell shops. He married Isabel Seavey, whose father was Alonzo Seavey, Jedediah's son. Their son Daniel (one of four sons and a daughter) died at the age of five from pneumonia. The following year, Peter died from complications of influenza contracted near the end of the great Spanish influenza epidemic. Isabel later remarried to Louis Cote, another machine shop worker.

OLIVER DYER B. APR 7, 1806 D. JUNE 13, 1872
OLIVE L. DREW B. NOV 22, 1811 D. SEPT 22, 1879

Oliver's grandfather Thomas Dyer married his neighbor Elizabeth Melchor in 1741. They lived on the Pool Road in Biddeford. Elizabeth gave birth to a number of children. All or most all of their female children survived and married, but by the time Oliver's father, Thomas, was born in 1769, they'd already lost in early childhood two sons they'd named Thomas, as well as one called Joseph to the bleeding disease hemophilia. (Hemophilia wasn't well understood until around the time that it appeared in the son of Queen Victoria, more than a century afterward; it would later, through Victoria's daughters, be famously passed to the family of the Russian tsar.)

That third Thomas Dyer had a middle name of Life, perhaps in an attempt to swing fate in a happier direction. Thomas survived long enough to marry Dorothy Foss and parent four children: John, Thomas, Abigail and Oliver. Thomas Life Dyer didn't die of hemophilia (and perhaps didn't even have the disease that's passed to about half a woman's sons), instead drowning at the age thirty-seven, when his son Oliver was only six months old. Records don't indicate what Dorothy did to support her small children—there were few career choices for a widow in the early nineteenth century.

Still a young boy, an impoverished Oliver moved to Boston and worked his way up in the business world. He married Olive L. Drew of Kennebunk. By the time he returned to Saco in midcentury, he was able to afford a large brick house at 19 Portland Road. He served on the city council and was elected mayor of Saco in 1871. Perhaps to end the long trail of childhood deaths, the Dyers had no children of their own but did adopt one son: Everard. Before Olive died seven years after her husband, she carefully crafted her will to make a remarkable philanthropic effort with the fortune Oliver had acquired. She donated $36,613 to open the Dyer Library, with just two restrictions: the money had to mostly be used for running the library (only $5,000 could be spent on a building) and her beloved husband's portrait had to hang there forever.

But there's a dark tale connected with the Dyer and Melchor families. It's said that in the late 1600s, a female member of the Melchor family jilted her betrothed, a pirate (of course). In revenge—the story goes—the pirate cast a curse on the family: from that time forward, none of the sons would live to bear children of their own. Since hemophilia is passed down through the female line by women who carry the trait (but aren't made ill by it), and whose sons suffer lethal consequences when they inherit it, the family definitely did carry some semblance of the legendary curse, even if not one cast by a pirate.

LEAVITT, E. HILL, D. 27 DEC 1869, AGED 67 YRS. 4 DAYS
CAROLINE A., WIFE OF E.H. 21 APR 1804–7 OCT 188[8?]
LAURA M., DAU. OF E. HILL AND CAROLINE A. LEAVITT, D. 13 MARCH 1872, AGED 35 YRS. 1 MO.
TOPPAN, D.L., 1832–1887
SARAH D., WIFE OF D.L. TOPPAN, DAU. OF E.H. AND C.A. LEAVITT, 14 APR 1834–4 JULY 1875
GEORGIA A., DAU OF D.L. AND S. D. TOPPAN, D. 4 SEPT 1869, AGED 2 YRS. 10 MOS.
IVY L., DAU. OF D.L. AND S.D. TOPPAN, D. 5 JUNE 1872, AGED 13 YRS.

Ebenezer Hill Leavitt worked as a "millman," or a worker in a mill. The family lived on Summer Street in Saco. The Leavitts had at least three children: Laura, born about 1829 and who died before the December 9, 1836 birth of Laura 2nd, who's buried here, and Sarah Deering Leavitt. Laura 2nd never moved away from her parents' home. On both the 1860 and 1870 censuses, she was working as a dressmaker.

Ebenezer died of "consumption" in 1869. When Laura died in 1872, it left her mother with no obvious source of income. Around that time, Caroline moved to Beach Street—perhaps a less expensive location—where she lived for the last few years of her life.

Sarah married Daniel Toppan—one of the few surviving children of George and Shuah Toppan. Daniel was a fairly successful farmer. However, John Haley—who was never a man to mince words—described Daniel as "the laziest man in town and simply died because even to breathe was a burden to him, so he, for a long time, only drew every other breath." Daniel and Sarah lived just a few houses down from Caroline on Beach Street. They had one other daughter besides the two buried here. Sarah died just three years after her daughter, thirteen-year-old Ivy.

MYRTLE AVENUE

WOOD, JAMES S., 1834–1926, CO. B, 12TH MAINE INFANTRY, G.A.R.
MERCY J. TEBBETTS, WIFE OF JAMES S. WOOD, 1830–1888
ANNIE M. 1855–1857
GEORGE S. 1857–1858
INFANT DAU., 1861–1861
CHARLES A. 1859–1893
JOHN S., 1857–1912
HORACE, 1844–1910
SALLY, WIFE OF AARON WOOD, D. 17 FEB 1849, AGED 77

Sally Perkins, the wife of Aaron Wood, was "of Hampton Falls, New Hampshire" when her marriage intentions to Aaron were published in September 1784. If her age at the time of her death was truly seventy-seven (as noted on her gravestone), then she was married at the age of just twelve or thirteen. By 1810, the Woods were living in Saco and had eight children in their household who were younger than sixteen. Of those young children, three would die over the course of just three days in April 1814. They died of a "spotted fever"—perhaps measles—that swept through Saco during late winter. Their youngest daughter, Rebecca, later married an Italian mariner, Michael Frangeni, and it's with this couple that brothers James, Charles and Horace Wood (probably sons of one of Rebecca's deceased older brothers) were living in 1850.

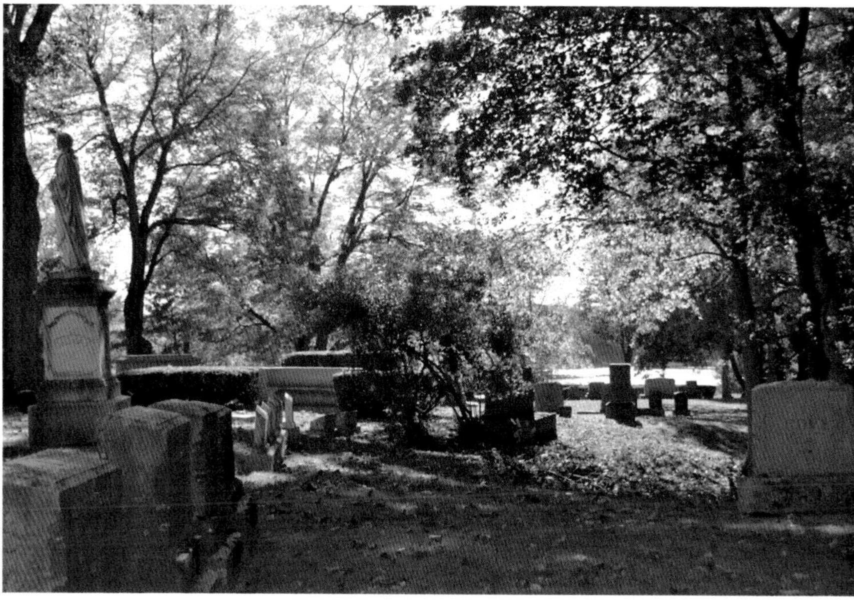

Laurel Hill Cemetery, "A place of resort." *Authors' collection.*

Although James worked as a hostler (taking care of horses) and later as a brick mason, he never achieved significant wealth. He enlisted in the Union army in November 1861 and served nearly to the end of the Civil War. Like many veterans of that conflict, afterward he joined the Grand Army of the Republic, the fraternal organization that was formed by former Union army members in 1866 and that, at its high-water mark, had 490,000 members. The GAR fought for soldiers' rights but was also a vibrant social club that organized annual national reunions and other more local events. It wasn't disbanded until the last member, a former drummer boy who lived to the age of 106, died in 1956. Of James Wood's children, only John—also a brick mason—lived well into adulthood. By the time of his death, James had moved to Portsmouth, where he died at the age of ninety-one.

Sally's gravestone was signed by its carver. It appears to say "A.E. Piper Saco," as does the stone of the Noyes children. Mr. Piper couldn't be identified.

BIBLIOGRAPHY

American Journal of the Medical Sciences, no. 9. New Series, January 1843. GoogleBooks, https://books.google.com/books?id=Xlg9AQAAMAAJ&pg=RA1-PR5&lpg=RA1-PR5&dq=yellow+fever+in+cuba+1842&source=bl&ots=S8nfuNL44y&sig=jfVmn_8GqJG4EWZRQZuK0FUdrf0&hl=en&sa=X&ved=0ahUKEwjRhpqRkMHWAhVG2mMKHfqhB48Q6AEINTAD#v=onepage&q=yellow%20fever%20in%20cuba%201842&f=false.

Biddeford Record 15, no. 239 (January 13, 1910).

Biographical Review: This Volume Contains Biographical Sketches of Leading Citizens of York County, Maine. Boston: Biographical Review Publishing Company, 1896.

Biographical Review of the Leading Citizens of York County, Maine. Boston: Biographical Review Publishing Company, 1896.

Blachowicz, James. *From Slate to Marble*. Vols. 1 and 2. Evanston, IL: Graver Press, 2015.

Bowdoin College Bulletin, no. 74. "Obituary Record of the Graduates of Bowdoin College for the Year Ending 1 June 1917" (May 1917). Bowdoin College, Brunswick, Maine.

Burnham, Edward P., and George A. Emery. *List of Students, 1813–1848: Thornton Academy, Saco, Maine*. Saco, ME: York Institute, 1918.

Early Vital Records of Massachusetts. Accessed at http://ma-vitalrecords.org.

Emery, Edwin, AM. *History of Sanford, Maine, 1661–1900*. Fall River, MA: William Morrell Emery, 1901.

First Book of Records of the Town of Pepperellborough Now the City of Saco. Portland, ME: Thurston Print, 1896.

Folsom, George. *History of Saco and Biddeford*. Portland: Maine Historical Society, 1975.

Gove, William, and Ira Gove. *The Gove Book: History and Genealogy of the American Family and Notes of European Goves*. Salem, MA: Sidney Perley, 1922.

Hamilton, Samuel King M.S. *The Hamiltons of Waterborough (York County, Maine), Their Ancestors and Descendants*. Boston: privately printed, 1912.

Hodgdon, George E. *Shannon Genealogy*. Rochester, NY: Foss Express Printing Company, 1905.

Hooper, Thomas, and Charles Henry Pope. *Hooper Genealogy*. Boston, MA: Charles H. Pope, 1908.

Howard, Cecil Hamden Cutts. *Genealogy of the Cutts Family of American*. Albany, NY: Joel Munsell's Sons, 1892.

Leland, Sherman. *The Leland Magazine, or a Genealogical Record of Henry Leland and His Descendants*. Boston: Wier & White, 1850.

Linden, Blanche M.G. *Silent City on a Hill: Picturesque Landscapes of Memory and Boston's Mount Auburn Cemetery*. Amherst: University of Massachusetts Press, 2007.

McIntyre, Philip W., and William F. Blanding, eds. *Men of Progress Maine Illustrated*. Boston: New England Magazine, 1897.

Romano, Ron. *Early Gravestones in Southern Maine*. Charleston, SC: The History Press, 2016.

Saco and Biddeford Directory, 1849. Saco, ME: L.O. Cowan and A.A. Hanscom, Publishers and Printers, 1849.

Whitman, William E.S., and Charles H. True. *Maine in the War for the Union*. Lewiston, ME: Nelson Dingley Jr. & Company, 1865.

INDEX

H

I

J

ABOUT THE AUTHORS

The executive director of the Dyer Library and Saco Museum, Leslie Rounds is an experienced author and historian who received a Master of Library Science degree from Southern Connecticut State University. She has written two books on schoolgirl embroidery to accompany exhibitions at the Saco Museum and is the co-author of a photographic book, *Saco Revisited*, for Arcadia Publishing's Images of America series. She has always been fascinated by the stories of people's lives.

Emory Rounds received his MA degree in history from Texas State University in 2010 and an MLIS from San Jose State University in 2017. He presently serves as the director of an academic library in southern Maine. In his spare time, he enjoys custom designing digital Lego models, writing steampunk and historical fiction novels, playing ball with his two border collies and watching BBC dramas.